Olney Hymns

By John Newton
This Edition Edited by Anthony Uyl

Devoted Publishing
Woodstock, Ontario, Canada 2018

Olney Hymns
Olney Hymns
By John Newton
This Edition Edited by Anthony Uyl

Originally Printed By: London: W. Oliver, 1779

The text of Olney Hymns is all in the Public Domain. The layout and Devoted Publishing logo are Copyright ©2018 Devoted Publishing. This edition is published by Devoted Publishing a division of 2165467 Ontario Inc.

**What kind of philosophies do you have?
Let us know!**

Visit our website: www.devotedpublishing.com
Contact us at: devotedpub@hotmail.com
Visit us on Facebook: @DevotedPublishing

Published in Woodstock, Ontario, Canada 2018.

For bulk educational rates, please contact us at the above email address.

ISBN: 978-1-77356-250-6

Table of Contents

OLNEY HYMNS, IN THREE BOOKS 9
PREFACE 10
BOOK I - On select Passages of Scripture 13
    GENESIS 13
    Hymn 1 13
    Hymn 2 15
    Hymn 3 16
    Hymn 4 17
    Hymn 5 18
    Hymn 6 19
    Hymn 7 20
    Hymn 8 22
    Hymn 9 24
    Hymn 10 26
    Hymn 11 27
    Hymn 12 28
    EXODUS 30
    Hymn 13 30
    Hymn 14 31
    Hymn 15 32
    Hymn 16 33
    Hymn 17 34
    Hymn 18 35
    LEVITICUS 36
    Hymn 19 36
    NUMBERS 38
    Hymn 20 38
    JOSHUA 39
    Hymn 21 39
    JUDGES 41
    Hymn 22 41
    Hymn 23 42
    Hymn 24 43
    I SAMUEL 44
    Hymn 25 44
    Footnotes: 45
    Hymn 26 46
    Hymn 27 47
    Hymn 28 48
    II SAMUEL 50
    Hymn 29 50
    Hymn 30 52
    I KINGS 53
    Hymn 31 53
    Hymn 32 54
    Hymn 33 55
    Hymn 34 56
    Hymn 35 58
    Footnotes: 59
    Hymn 36 60
    II KINGS 61
    Hymn 37 61
    Hymn 38 63
    Hymn 39 65
    Hymn 40 66
    I CHRONICLES 67
    Hymn 41 67
    NEHEMIAH 68
    Hymn 42 68
    JOB 69
    Hymn 43 69
    Hymn 44 71
    Footnotes: 72
    PSALMS 73
    Hymn 45 73
    Hymn 46 74
    Hymn 47 75
    Hymn 48 76
    Hymn 49 77
    Hymn 50 78
    Footnotes: 78
    Hymn 51 79
    PROVERBS 81
    Hymn 52 81
    Hymn 53 82
    Hymn 54 84

Olney Hymns

Footnotes:	84
Hymn 55	85
Hymn 56	86
SONG OF SOLOMON	87
Hymn 57	87
ISAIAH	88
Hymn 58	88
Hymn 59	89
Hymn 60	90
Footnotes:	91
Hymn 61	92
Hymn 62	94
Hymn 63	96
Hymn 64	98
Hymn 65	99
JEREMIAH	100
Hymn 66	100
Hymn 67	101
Hymn 68	102
LAMENTATIONS	103
Hymn 69	103
Footnotes:	103
EZEKIEL	104
Hymn 70	104
Hymn 71	106
Hymn 72	107
DANIEL	108
Hymn 73	108
Hymn 74	110
JONAH	111
Hymn 75	111
ZECHARIAH	112
Hymn 76	112
Hymn 77	113
Hymn 78	114
Hymn 79	116
MALACHI	117
Hymn 80	117
MATTHEW	118
Hymn 81	118
Hymn 82	120
Hymn 83	121
Hymn 84	122
Hymn 85	123
Hymn 86	124
Hymn 87	125
Hymn 88	126
Hymn 89	127
Hymn 90	129
Footnotes:	130
Hymn 91	131
MARK	133
Hymn 92	133
Footnotes:	134
Hymn 93	135
Hymn 94	137
Footnotes:	137
Hymn 95	138
Hymn 96	139
Hymn 97	140
LUKE	141
Hymn 98	141
Hymn 99	143
Hymn 100	144
Hymn 101	145
Hymn 102	146
Hymn 103	147
Footnotes:	148
Hymn 104	149
Hymn 105	150
Hymn 106	152
Footnotes:	153
Hymn 107	154
Hymn 108	156
Hymn 109	157
Hymn 110	158
JOHN	159
Hymn 111	159

Hymn 112	161
Footnotes:	162
Hymn 113	163
Footnotes:	164
Hymn 114	165
Footnotes:	166
Hymn 115	167
Hymn 116	168
Hymn 117	169
Hymn 118	170
Hymn 119	171
ACTS	173
Hymn 120	173
Hymn 121	174
Hymn 122	176
Hymn 123	178
Hymn 124	179
Hymn 125	180
ROMANS	181
Hymn 126	181
Hymn 127	183
I CORINTHIANS	184
Hymn 128	184
II CORINTHIANS	185
Hymn 129	185
GALATIANS	186
Hymn 130	186
PHILIPPIANS	188
Hymn 131	188
Footnotes:	189
HEBREWS	190
Hymn 132	190
Hymn 133	192
Hymn 134	193
Hymn 135	194
REVELATION	195
Hymn 136	195
Hymn 137	196
Hymn 138	197
Hymn 139	198
Hymn 140	199
Hymn 141	200
Footnotes:	200
BOOK II	201
I. SEASONS	201
Hymn 1	201
Hymn 2	202
Hymn 3	203
Hymn 4	204
Hymn 5	206
Hymn 6	208
HYMNS before annual Sermons to young people, on new-years evenings.	210
Hymn 7	210
Hymn 8	211
Hymn 9	212
Hymn 10	213
Hymn 11	214
Hymn 12	215
Hymn 13	216
Hymn 14	217
Hymn 15	218
Hymn 16	219
Hymn 17	221
Hymn 18	222
Hymn 19	223
HYMNS after Sermons to young people, on new-years evenings, suited to the subjects	224
Hymn 20	224
Hymn 21	225
Hymn 22	226
Hymn 23	227
Hymn 24	228
Hymn 25	229
Hymn 26	230
Hymn 27	232
Hymn 28	233

Olney Hymns

Hymn 29	234
Hymn 30	235
Footnotes:	235
Hymn 31	236
Hymn 32	237
Hymn 33	239
Footnotes:	240
Hymn 34	241
Footnotes:	242
Hymn 35	243
Hymn 36	244
CHRISTMAS	246
Hymn 37	246
Hymn 38	247
Hymn 39	248
Footnotes:	248
Hymn 40	249
THE CLOSE OF THE YEAR	250
Hymn 41	250
Hymn 42	252
II. ORDINANCES	254
Hymn 43	254
Hymn 44	255
Hymn 45	256
Hymn 46	257
Hymn 47	258
Hymn 48	259
Footnotes:	259
Hymn 49	260
Hymn 50	262
Hymn 51	263
Hymn 52	265
SACRAMENTAL HYMNS	266
Hymn 53	266
Hymn 54	267
Hymn 55	268
Hymn 56	269
Hymn 57	270
Hymn 58	271
Hymn 59	272
ON PRAYER	273
Hymn 60	273
Hymn 61	274
ON THE SCRIPTURE	275
Hymn 62	275
Hymn 63	276
III. PROVIDENCES	277
Hymn 64	277
Footnotes:	278
FAST-DAY HYMNS	279
Hymn 65	279
Hymn 66	281
Hymn 67	282
Hymn 68	283
Hymn 69	284
Hymn 70	285
Hymn 71	286
FUNERAL HYMNS	287
Hymn 72	287
Hymn 73	289
Hymn 74	290
Hymn 75	291
Hymn 76	292
Hymn 77	293
Hymn 78	294
Footnotes:	294
Hymn 79	295
IV. CREATION	297
Hymn 80	297
Hymn 81	298
Hymn 82	299
Hymn 83	300
Hymn 84	301
Hymn 85	302
Hymn 86	303
Hymn 87	304
Footnotes:	305
Hymn 88	306

Hymn 89	307	Hymn 23	349
Hymn 90	308	Hymn 24	350
Hymn 91	309	Hymn 25	351
Footnotes:	309	Hymn 26	353
Hymn 92	310	Hymn 27	354
Hymn 93	311	Hymn 28	355
Hymn 94	312	Hymn 29	356
Hymn 95	313	Hymn 30	357
Hymn 96	314	Hymn 31	359
Hymn 97	315	Hymn 32	360
Hymn 98	316	Hymn 33	361
Hymn 99	317	Hymn 34	362
Hymn 100	318	Hymn 35	363
BOOK III	319	Hymn 36	364
I. Solemn Addresses to Sinners	319	Hymn 37	365
Hymn 1	319	Hymn 38	367
Hymn 2	321	Hymn 39	369
Hymn 3	323	Hymn 40	370
Hymn 4	325	Hymn 41	371
Hymn 5	327	Hymn 42	372
II. Seeking, Pleading, and Hoping	329	IV. COMFORT	373
Hymn 6	329	Hymn 43	373
Hymn 7	331	Hymn 44	374
Hymn 8	333	Hymn 45	375
Hymn 9	334	Hymn 46	376
Hymn 10	336	Hymn 47	377
Hymn 11	337	Hymn 48	378
Hymn 12	338	Hymn 49	379
Hymn 13	339	Hymn 50	380
Hymn 14	340	Hymn 51	381
III. CONFLICT	341	Hymn 52	382
Hymn 15	341	Hymn 53	383
Hymn 16	342	Hymn 54	384
Hymn 17	343	Hymn 55	385
Hymn 18	344	Hymn 56	386
Hymn 19	345	Hymn 57	388
Hymn 20	346	Hymn 58	389
Hymn 21	347	V. DEDICATION and SURRENDER	390
Hymn 22	348		

Olney Hymns

Hymn 59	390
Hymn 60	391
Hymn 61	392
Hymn 62	393
Hymn 63	394
Hymn 64	395
Hymn 65	396
Hymn 66	397
Hymn 67	398
VI. CAUTIONS	399
Hymn 68	399
Hymn 69	400
Hymn 70	401
Hymn 71	402
Hymn 72	403
Hymn 73	404
Hymn 74	405
Hymn 75	406
Hymn 76	407
Hymn 77	408
Hymn 78	409
Hymn 79	410
VII. PRAISE	411
Hymn 80	411
Hymn 81	412
Hymn 82	413
Hymn 83	415
Hymn 84	416
Hymn 85	417
Hymn 86	418
Hymn 87	420
Hymn 88	422
VIII. SHORT HYMNS: BEFORE SERMON	423
Hymn 89	423
Hymn 90	424
Hymn 91	425
Hymn 92	426
Hymn 93	427
Hymn 94	428
Hymn 95	429
AFTER SERMON	430
Hymn 96	430
Hymn 97	431
Hymn 98	432
Hymn 99	433
Hymn 100	434
Hymn 101	435
Hymn 102	436
Hymn 103	437
GLORIA PATRIA	438
Hymn 104	438
Hymn 105	439
Hymn 106	440
Hymn 107	441

OLNEY HYMNS, IN THREE BOOKS

    Book I. On select Texts of Scripture.
    Book II. On occasional Subjects.
    Book III. On the Progress and Changes of the Spiritual Life.

--Cantabitis, Arcades, inquit, Montibus haec vestris: foli cantare periti Arcades. O mihi tum quam molliter ossa quiescant Vestra meos olim si fistula dicat amores! Virgil, Ecl. x:31.

    And they sang as it were a new song before the throne;--and no man could learn that song, but the redeemed from the earth. Rev. 14:3.

    As sorrowful--yet always rejoicing, 2 Cor. 6:10.

PREFACE

Copies of a few of these Hymns have already appeared in periodical publications, and in some recent collections. I have observed one or two of them attributed to persons who certainly had no concern in them, but as transcribers. All that have been at different times parted with in manuscript are included in the present volume; and (if the information were of any great importance) the public may be assured, that the whole number were composed by two persons only. The original design would not admit of any other association. A desire of promoting the faith and comfort of sincere christians, though the principal, was not the only motive to this undertaking. It was likewise intended as a monument, to perpetuate the remembrance of an intimate and endeared friendship. With this pleasing view I entered upon my part, which would have been smaller than it is, and the book would have appeared much sooner, and in a very different form, if the wise, though mysterious providence of GOD, had not seen fit to cross my wishes. We had not proceeded far upon our proposed plan, before my dear friend was prevented, by a long and affecting indisposition, from affording me any farther assistance. My grief and disappointment were great; I hung my harp upon the willows, and for some time thought myself determined to proceed no farther without him. Yet my mind was afterwards led to resume the service. My progress in it, amidst a variety of other engagements, has been slow, yet in a course of years the hymns amounted to a considerable number: And my deference to the judgment and desires of others, has at length overcome the reluctance I long felt to see them in print, while I had so few of my friend's hymns to insert in the collection. Though it is possible a good judge of composition might be able to distinguish those which are his, I have thought it proper to preclude a misapplication, by prefixing the letter C to each of them. For the rest, I must be responsible. [Note: in the electronic edition, each hymn is given a full, specific ascription.]

There is a style and manner suited to the composition of hymns, which may be more successfully, or at least more easily attained by a versifier, than by a poet. They should be Hymns, not Odes, if designed for public worship, and for the use of plain people. Perspicuity, simplicity and ease, should be chiefly attended to; and the imagery and coloring of poetry, if admitted at all, should be indulged very sparingly and with great judgment. The late Dr. Watts, many of whose hymns are admirable patterns in this species of writing, might, as a poet, have a right to say, That it cost him some labor to restrain his fire, and to accommodate himself to the capacities of common readers. But it would not become me to make such a declaration. It behoved me to do my best. But though I would not offend readers of taste by a wilful coarseness, and negligence, I do not write professedly for them. If the LORD whom I serve, has been pleased to favor me with that mediocrity of talent, which may qualify me for usefulness to the weak and the poor of his flock, without quite disgusting persons of superior discernment, I have reason to be satisfied.

John Newton

As the workings of the heart of man, and of the Spirit of God, are in general the same, in all who are the subjects of grace, I hope most of these hymns, being the fruit and expression of my own experience, will coincide with the views of real christians of all denominations. But I cannot expect that every sentiment I have advanced will be universally approved. However, I am not conscious of having written a single line with an intention, either to flatter, or to offend any party or person upon earth. I have simply declared my own views and feelings, as I might have done if I had composed hymns in some of the newly discovered islands in the South-Sea, where no person had any knowledge of the name of Jesus, but myself. I am a friend of peace, and being deeply convinced that no one can profitably understand the great truths and doctrines of the gospel, any farther than he is taught of God, I have not a wish to obtrude my own tenets upon others, in a way of controversy: yet I do not think myself bound to conceal them. Many gracious persons (for many such I am persuaded there are) who differ from me, more or less, in those points which are called Calvinistic, appear desirous that the Calvinists should, for their sakes, studiously avoid every expression which they cannot approve. Yet few of them, I believe. impose a like restraint upon themselves, but think the importance of what they deem to be truth, justifies them in speaking their sentiments plainly, and strongly. May I not plead for an equal liberty? The views I have received of the doctrines of grace are essential to my peace, I could not live comfortably a day or an hour without them. I likewise believe, yea, so far as my poor attainments warrant me to speak, I know them to be friendly to holiness, and to have a direct influence in producing and maintaining a gospel conversation, and therefore I must not be ashamed of them.

The Hymns are distributed into three Books. In the first I have classed those which are formed upon select passages of Scripture, and placed them in the order of the books of the old and New Testament. The second contains occasional Hymns, suited to particular seasons, or suggested by particular events or objects. The third Book is miscellaneous, comprising a variety of subjects relative to a life of faith in the son of God, which have no express reference either to a single text of Scripture, or to any determinate season or incident. These are farther subdivided into distinct heads. This arrangement is not so accurate but that several of the hymns might have been differently disposed. Some attention to method may be found convenient, though a logical exactness was hardly practicable. As some subjects in the several books are nearly co-incident, I have, under the divisions in the third book, pointed out those which are similar in the two former. And I have likewise here and there in the first and second, made a reference to hymns of a like import in the third.

This publication, which, with my humble prayer to the LORD for his blessing upon it, I offer to the service and acceptance of all who love the LORD JESUS CHRIST in sincerity, of every name and in every place, into whose hands it may come; I more particularly dedicate to my dear friends in the parish and neighborhood of Olney, for whose use the hymns were originally composed; as a testimony of the sincere love I bear them, and as a token of my gratitude to the Lord, and to them, for the comfort and satisfaction with which the discharge of my ministry among them has been attended.

The hour is approaching, and at my time of life cannot be very distant, when my heart, my pen, and my tongue, will no longer be able to move in their

Olney Hymns

service. But I trust, while my heart continues to beat, it will feel a warm desire for the prosperity of their souls; and while my hand can write, and my tongue speak, it will be the business and the pleasure of my life, to aim at promoting their growth and establishment in the grace of our God and Savior. To this precious grace I commend them, and earnestly entreat them, and all who love his name, to strive mightily with their prayers to God for me, that I may be preserved faithful to the end, and enabled at last to finish my course with joy. Olney, Bucks,

    Feb. 15, 1779
    JOHN NEWTON.

BOOK I – On select Passages of Scripture

GENESIS

Hymn 1
John Newton
ADAM. Gen 3:9

On man, in his own image made,
How much did GOD bestow?
The whole creation homage paid,
And owned him LORD, below!

He dwelt in Eden's garden, stored
With sweets for every sense;
And there with his descending LORD
He walked in confidence.

But O! by sin how quickly changed!
His honor forfeited,
His heart, from God and truth, estranged,
His conscience filled with dread!

Now from his Maker's voice he flees,
Which was before his joy:
And thinks to hide, amidst the trees,
From an All-seeing eye.

Compelled to answer to his name,
With stubbornness and pride
He cast, on God himself, the blame,
Nor once for mercy cried.

But grace, unasked, his heart subdued
And all his guilt forgave;
By faith, the promised seed he viewed,
And felt his pow'r to save.

Thus we ourselves would justify,
Though we the Law transgress;
Like him, unable to deny,

Olney Hymns
Unwilling to confess.

But when by faith the sinner sees
A pardon bought with blood;
Then he forsakes his foolish pleas,
And gladly turns to God.

Hymn 2
John Newton
CAIN and ABEL. Gen 4:3-8

When Adam fell he quickly lost
God's image, which he once possessed:
See All our nature since could boast
In Cain, his first-born Son, expressed!

The sacrifice the Lord ordained
In type of the Redeemer's blood,
Self-righteous reas'ning Cain disdained,
And thought his own first-fruits as good.

Yet rage and envy filled his mind,
When, with a fallen, downcast look,
He saw his brother favor find,
Who GOD's appointed method took.

By Cain's own hand, good Abel died,
Because the Lord approved his faith;
And, when his blood for vengeance cried,
He vainly thought to hide his death.

Such was the wicked murd'rer Cain,
And such by nature still are we,
Until by grace we're born again,
Malicious, blind and proud, as he.

Like him the way of grace we slight,
And in our own devices trust;
Call evil good, and darkness light,
And hate and persecute the just.

The saints, in every age and place,
Have found this history fulfilled;
The numbers all our thoughts surpass
Of Abels, whom the Cains have killed!
Rom 8:36

Thus JESUS fell--but O! his blood
Far better things than Abel's cries:
Heb 12:24
Obtains his murd'rers peace with God,
And gains them mansions in the skies.

Hymn 3
William Cowper
Walking with GOD. Gen 5:24

O! for a closer walk with God,
A calm and heav'nly frame;
A light to shine upon the road
That leads me to the Lamb!

Where is the blessedness I knew
When first I saw the LORD?
Where is the soul-refreshing view
Of JESUS, and his word?

What peaceful hours I once enjoyed!
How sweet their memory still!
But they have left an aching void,
The world can never fill.

Return, O holy Dove, return,
Sweet messenger of rest;
I hate the sins that made thee mourn,
And drove thee from my breast.

The dearest idol I have known,
Whate'er that idol be;
Help me to tear it from thy throne,
And worship only thee.

So shall my walk be close with God,
Calm and serene my frame;
So purer light shall mark the road
That leads me to the Lamb.

Hymn 4
John Newton
Walking with GOD.

By faith in CHRIST I walk with God,
With heav'n, my journeys'-end, in view;
Supported by his staff and rod,
Ps 23:4
My road is safe and pleasant too,

I travel through a desert wide
Where many round me blindly stray;
Ps 107:7
But He vouchsafes to be my guide,
And will not let me miss my way.

Though snares and dangers throng my path,
And earth and hell my course withstand;
I triumph over all by faith,
Ps 27:1,2
Guarded by his Almighty hand.

The wilderness affords no food,
But God for my support prepares;
Provides me every needful good,
And frees my soul from wants and cares.

With him sweet converse I maintain,
Great as he is I dare be free;
I tell him all my grief and pain,
And he reveals his love to me.

Some cordial from his word he brings,
Whene'er my feeble spirit faints;
At once my soul revives and sings,
And yields no more to sad complaints.

I pity all that worldlings talk
Of pleasures that will quickly end;
Be this my choice, O Lord, to walk
With thee, my Guide, my Guard, my Friend.

Hymn 5
John Newton
Lot in Sodom.
Gen 13:10

How hurtful was the choice of Lot,
Who took up his abode
(Because it was a fruitful spot)
With them who feared not God!

A pris'ner he was quickly made,
Bereaved of all his store;
And, but for Abraham's timely aid,
He had returned no more.

Yet still he seemed resolved to stay
As if it were his rest;
Although their sins from day to day
His righteous soul distressed.
2 Peter 2:8

Awhile he stayed with anxious mind,
Exposed to scorn and strife;
At last he left his all behind,
And fled to save his life.

In vain his sons-in-law he warned,
They thought he told his dreams;
His daughters too, of them had learned,
And perished in the flames.

His wife escaped a little way,
But died for looking back:
Does not her case to pilgrims say,
"Beware of growing slack?"

Yea; Lot himself could ling'ring stand,
Though vengeance was in view;
'Twas mercy plucked him by the hand,
Or he had perished too.

The doom of Sodom wilt be ours
If to the earth we cleave;
Lord quicken all our drowsy pow'rs,
To flee to thee and live.

John Newton

Hymn 6
William Cowper
JEHOVAH-JIREH,
The LORD will provide.
Gen 22:14

The saints should never be dismayed,
Nor sink in hopeless fear;
For when they least expect his aid,
The Savior will appear.

This Abraham found, he raised the knife,
GOD saw, and said, "Forbear;"
Yon ram shall yield his meaner life,
Behold the victim there.

Once David seemed Saul's certain prey,
But hark! the foe's at hand;
1Sam 23:27
Saul turns his arms another way,
To save th' invaded land.

When Jonah sunk beneath the wave
He thought to rise no more;
Jonah 1:17
But God prepared a fish to save,
And bear him to the shore.

Blest proofs of pow'r and grace divine,
That meet us in his word!
May every deep-felt care of mine
Be trusted with the Lord.

Wait for his seasonable aid,
And though it tarry wait:
The promise may be long-delayed,
But cannot come too late.

Hymn 7
John Newton
The LORD will provide.

Though troubles assail
And dangers affright,
Though friends should all fail
And foes all unite;
Yet one thing secures us,
Whatever betide,
The scripture assures us,
The Lord will provide.

The birds without barn
Or storehouse are fed,
From them let us learn
To trust for our bread:
His saints, what is fitting,
Shall ne'er he denied,
So long as 'tis written,
The Lord will provide.

We may, like the ships,
By tempest be tossed
On perilous deeps,
But cannot be lost.
Though Satan enrages
The wind and the tide,
The promise engages,
The Lord will provide.

His call we obey
Like Abram of old,
Not knowing our way,
But faith makes us bold;
For though we are strangers
We have a good Guide,
And trust in all dangers,
The Lord will provide.

When Satan appears
To stop up our path,
And fill us with fears,
We triumph by faith;
He cannot take from us,

John Newton

Though oft he has tried,
This heart-cheering promise,
The Lord will provide.

He tells us we're weak,
Our hope is in vain,
The good that we seek
We ne'er shall obtain,
But when such suggestions
Our spirits have plied,
This answers all questions,
The Lord will provide.

No strength of our own,
Or goodness we claim,
Yet since we have known
The Savior's great name;
In this our strong tower
For safety we hide,
The Lord is our power,
The Lord will provide.

When life sinks apace
And death is in view,
This word of his grace
Shall comfort us through:
No fearing or doubting
With Christ on our side,
We hope to die shouting,
The Lord will provide.

Hymn 8
John Newton
ESAU
Gen 25:34; Heb 12:16

Poor Esau repented too late
That once he his birth-right despised;
And sold, for a morsel of meat,
What could not too highly be prized:
How great was his anguish when told,
The blessing he sought to obtain,
Was gone with the birth-right he sold,
And none could recall it again!

He stands as a warning to all,
Wherever the gospel shall come;
O Hasten and yield to the call,
While yet for repentance there's room!
Your season will quickly be past,
Then hear and obey it today;
Lest when you seek mercy at last,
The Savior should frown you away.

What is it the world can propose?
A morsel of meat at the best!
For this are you willing to lose
A share in the joys of the blest?
Its pleasures will speedily end,
Its favor and praise are but breath;
And what can its profits befriend
Your soul in the moment of death?

If Jesus for these you despise,
And sin to the Savior prefer;
In vain your entreaties and cries,
When summoned to stand at his bar:
How will you his presence abide?
What anguish will torture your heart?
The saints all enthroned by his side,
And you be compelled to depart.

Too often, dear Savior, have I
Preferred some poor trifle to thee;
How is it thou dost not deny
The blessing and birth-right to me?

John Newton

No better than Esau I am,
Though pardon and heav'n be mine;
To me belongs nothing but shame,
The praise and the glory be thine.

Hymn 9
John Newton
Jacob's Ladder
Gen 28:12

If the LORD our leader be,
We may follow without fear;
East or West, by land or sea,
Home, with him, is everywhere;
When from Esau Jacob fled,
Though his pillow was a stone,
And the ground his humble bed,
Yet he was not left alone.

Kings are often waking kept,
Racked with cares on beds of state;
Never king like Jacob slept.
For he lay at heaven's gate:
Lo! he saw a ladder reared,
Reaching to the heav'nly throne;
At the top the Lord appeared,
Spake and claimed him for his own.

"Fear not, Jacob, thou art mine,
And my presence with thee goes;
On thy heart my love shall shine,
And my arm subdue thy foes:
From my promise comfort take;
For my help in trouble call;
Never will I thee forsake,
'Till I have accomplished all."

Well does Jacob's ladder suit
To the gospel throne of grace;
We are at the ladder's foot,
Every hour, in every place
By affirming flesh and blood,
JESUS heav'n and earth unites;
We by faith ascend to God,
2Cor 6:16
God to dwell with us delights.

They who know the Savior's name,
Are for all events prepared
What can changes do to them,

John Newton

Who have such a Guide and Guard?
Should they traverse earth around,
To the ladder still they come;
Every spot is holy ground,
God is there--and he's their home,

Hymn 10
John Newton
My name is JACOB.
Gen 32:27

Nay, I cannot let Thee go,
Till a blessing thou bestow;
Do not turn away thy face,
Mine's an urgent pressing case.

Dost thou ask me, who I am?
Ah, my LORD, thou know'st my name!
Yet the question gives a plea,
To support my suit with thee.

Thou didst once a wretch behold,
In rebellion blindly bold;
Scorn thy grace, thy pow'r defy,
That poor rebel, Lord, was I.

Once a sinner near despair,
Sought thy mercy-seat by prayer;
Mercy heard and set him free,
Lord, that mercy came to me.

Many years have passed since then,
Many changes I have seen;
Yet have been upheld till now,
Who could hold me up but thou?

Thou hast helped in every need,
This emboldens me to plead;
After so much mercy past,
Canst thou let me sink at last?

No--I must maintain my hold,
'Tis thy goodness makes me bold;
I can no denial take,
When I plead for Jesu's sake.

Hymn 11
John Newton
Plenty in a time of dearth.
Gen 41:56

My soul once had its plenteous years,
And throve, with peace and comfort filled,
Like the fat kine and ripened ears,
Which Pharaoh in his dream beheld.

With pleasing frames and grace received,
With means and ordinances fed;
How happy for a while I lived,
And little feared the want of bread.

But famine came and left no sign,
Of all the plenty I had seen;
Like the dry ears and half-starved kine,
I then looked withered, faint and lean.

To Joseph the Egyptians went,
To Jesus I made known my case;
He, when my little stock was spent,
Opened his magazine of grace.

For he the time of dearth foresaw,
And made provision long before;
That famished souls, like me, might draw
Supplies from his unbounded store.

Now on his bounty I depend,
And live from fear of dearth secure,
Maintained by such a mighty friend,
I cannot want till he is poor.

O sinners hear his gracious call!
His mercy's door stands open wide,
He has enough to feed you all,
And none who come shall be denied.

Hymn 12
John Newton
Joseph made known to his Brethren.
Gen 45:3,4

When Joseph his brethren beheld,
Afflicted and trembling with fear;
His heart with compassion was filled,
From weeping he could not forbear.
Awhile his behavior was rough,
To bring their past sin to their mind;
But when they were humbled enough,
He hasted to show himself kind.

How little they thought it was he,
Whom they had ill treated and sold!
How great their confusion must be,
As soon as his name he had told!
"I am Joseph, your brother, he said,
And still to my heart you are dear,
You sold me, and thought I was dead,
But God, for your sakes, sent me here."

Though greatly distressed before,
When charged with purloining the cup;
They now were confounded much more,
Not one of them durst to look up.
"Can Joseph, whom we would have slain.
Forgive us the evil we did?
And will he our households maintain?
O this is a brother indeed!"

Thus dragged by my conscience, I came,
And laden with guilt, to the Lord;
Surrounded with terror and shame,
Unable to utter a word.
At first he looked stern and revere,
What anguish then pierced my heart!
Expecting each moment to hear
The sentence, "Thou cursed, depart!"

But O! what surprise when he spoke,
While tenderness beamed in his face;
My heart then to pieces was broke,
O'erwhelmed and confounded by grace:

John Newton

"Poor sinner, I know thee full well,
By thee I was sold and was slain;
But I died to redeem thee from hell,
And raise thee in glory to reign.

I am JESUS, whom thou hast blasphemed,
And crucified often afresh;
But let me henceforth be esteemed,
Thy brother, thy bone, and thy flesh:
My pardon I freely bestow,
Thy wants I will fully supply;
I'll guide thee and guard thee below,
And soon will remove thee on high.

Go, publish to sinners around,
That they may be willing to come,
The mercy which now you have found,
And tell them that yet there is room."
O, sinners, the message obey!
No more vain excuses pretend;
But come, without farther delay,
To Jesus our brother and friend.

EXODUS

Hymn 13
John Newton
The Bitter waters.
Ex 15:23-15

Bitter, indeed, the waters are.
Which in this desert flow;
Though to the eye they promise fair,
They taste of sin and woe.

Of pleasing draughts I once could dream,
But now, awake, l find,
That sin has poisoned every stream,
And left a curse behind.

But there's a wonder-working wood,
I've heard believers say,
Can make these bitter waters good,
And take the curse away.

The virtues of this healing tree
Are known and prized by few;
Reveal this secret, Lord, to me,
That I may prize it too.

The cross on which the Savior died,
And conquered for his saints;
This is the tree, by faith applied,
Which sweetens all complaints.

Thousands have found the blest effect,
Nor longer mourn their lot;
While on his sorrows they reflect,
Their own are all forgot.

When they, by faith, behold the cross,
Though many griefs they meet;
They draw again from every loss,
And find the bitter sweet.

Hymn 14
William Cowper
JEHOVAH-ROPHI,
I am the Lord that healeth thee.
Ex 15

Heal us, EMMANUEL, here we are,
Waiting to feel thy touch;
Deep wounded souls to thee repair,
And, Savior we are such.

Our faith is feeble we confess,
We faintly trust thy word;
But wilt thou pity us the less?
Be that far from thee, Lord!

Remember him who once applied
With trembling for relief;
"Lord, I believe, with tears he cried,
O help my unbelief."
Mk 9:24

She too, who touched thee in the press,
And healing virtue stole;
Was answered, "Daughter, go in peace,
Thy faith hath made thee whole."
Mk 5:34

Concealed amid the gath'ring throng,
She would have shunned thy view;
And if her faith was firm and strong,
Had strong misgivings too.

Like her, with hopes and fears, we come,
To touch thee if we may;
O! send us not despairing home,
Send none unhealed away.

Hymn 15
John Newton
MANNA.
Ex 16:18

Manna to Israel well supplied
The want of other bread;
While God is able to provide,
His people shall be fed.

(Thus though the corn and wine should fail,
And creature-streams be dry;
The prayer of faith will still prevail,
For blessings from on high.)

Of his kind care how sweet a proof!
It suited every taste;
Who gathered most, had just enough,
Enough, who gathered least.

'Tis thus our gracious Lord provides
Our comforts and our cares;
His own unerring hand provides,
And gives us each our shares.

He knows how much the weak can bear,
And helps them when they cry;
The strongest have no strength to spare,
For such he'll strongly try.

Daily they saw the Manna come,
And cover all the ground;
But what they tried to keep at home,
Corrupted soon was found.

Vain their attempt to store it up,
This was to tempt the Lord;
Israel must live by faith and hope,
And not upon a hoard.

Hymn 16
John Newton
Manna hoarded.
Ex 16:20

The manna favored Israel's meat,
Was gathered day by day;
When all the host was served, the heat
Melted the rest away.

In vain to hoard it up they tried,
Against tomorrow came;
It then bred worms and putrefied,
And proved their sin and shame.

'Twas daily bread and would not keep,
But must be still renewed;
Faith should not want a hoard or heap,
But trust the LORD for food.

The truths by which the soul is fed,
Must thus be had afresh;
For notions resting in the head,
Will only feed the flesh.

However true, they have no life,
Or unction to impart;
They breed the worms of pride and strife,
But cannot cheer the heart.

Nor can the best experience past,
The life of faith maintain;
The brightest hope will faint at last,
Unless supplied again.

Dear Lord, while we in prayer are found,
Do thou the Manna give;
O! let it fall on all around,
That we may eat and live.

Hymn 17
William Cowper
JEHOVAH-NISSI,
The Lord my banner.
Ex 17:15

By whom was David taught,
To aim the dreadful blow,
When he Goliath fought,
And laid the Gittite low?
No sword nor spear the stripling took,
But chose a pebble from the brook.

'Twas Israel's God and king,
Who sent him to the fight;
Who gave him strength to fling,
And skill to aim aright.
Ye feeble saints your strength endures,
Because young David's GOD is yours.

Who ordered Gideon forth,
To storm th' invaders' camp,
Judg 7:20
With arms of little worth,
A pitcher and a lamp?
The trumpets made his coming known,
And all the host was overthrown.

Oh! I have seen the day,
When with a single word,
GOD helping me to say,
My trust is in the LORD;
My soul has quelled a thousand foes,
Fearless of all that could oppose.

But unbelief, self-will,
Self-righteousness and pride,
How often do they steal
My weapon from my side?
Yet David's LORD, and Gideon's friend,
Will help his servant to the end.

Hymn 18

John Newton
The golden calf.
Ex 32:4,31

When Israel heard the fiery law,
From Sinai's top proclaimed;
Their hearts seemed full of holy awe,
Their stubborn spirits tamed.

Yet, as forgetting all they knew,
Ere forty days were past;
With blazing Sinai still in view,
A molten calf they cast.

Yea, Aaron, God's anointed priest,
Who on the mount had been
He durst prepare the idol-beast,
And lead them on to sin.

LORD, what is man! and what are we,
To recompense thee thus!
In their offence our own we see,
Their story points at us.

From Sinai we have heard thee speak,
And from mount Calv'ry too;
And yet to idols oft we seek,
While thou art in our view.

Some golden calf, or golden dream,
Some fancied creature-good,
Presumes to share the heart with him,
Who bought the whole with blood.

LORD, save us from our golden calves,
Our sin with grief we own;
We would no more be thine by halves,
But live to thee alone.

LEVITICUS

Hymn 19
John Newton
The true AARON
Lev 8:7-9

See Aaron, God's anointed priest,
Within the veil appear;
In robes of mystic meaning dressed,
Presenting Israel's prayer.

The plate of gold which crowns his brows,
His holiness describes;
His breast displays, in shining rows,
The names of all the tribes.

With the atoning blood he stands,
Before the mercy-seat;
And clouds of incense from his hands,
Arise with odor sweet.

Urim and Thummim near his heart,
In rich engravings worn;
The sacred light of truth impart,
To teach and to adorn.

Through him the eye of faith descries,
A greater Priest than he;
Thus JESUS pleads above the skies,
For you, my friends, and me.

He bears the names of all his saints,
Deep on his heart engraved;
Attentive to the state and wants
Of all his love has saved.

In him a holiness complete,
Light and perfections shine;
And wisdom, grace, and glory meet;
A Savior all divine.

The blood, which as a Priest he bears
For sinners, is his own

John Newton

The incense of his prayers and tears
Perfume the holy throne.

In him my weary soul has rest,
Though I am weak and vile
I read my name upon his breast,
And see the Father smile.

NUMBERS

Hymn 20
John Newton
BALAAM's wish
Num 23:10

How blest the righteous are
When they resign their breath!
No wonder Balaam wished to share
In such a happy death.

"Oh! let me die, said he,
The death the righteous do;
When life is ended let me be
Found with the faithful few."

The force of truth how great!
When enemies confess,
None but the righteous whom they hate,
A solid hope possess.

But Balaam's wish was vain,
His heart was insincere;
He thirsted for unrighteous gain,
And sought a portion here.

He seemed the LORD to know,
And to offend him loth;
But Mammon proved his overthrow,
For none can serve them both.

May you, my friends, and I,
Warning from hence receive;
If like the righteous we would die,
To choose the life they live.

JOSHUA

Hymn 21
John Newton
GIBEON.
Josh 10:6

When Joshua, by GOD's command,
Invaded Canaan's guilty land;
Gibeon, unlike the nations round,
Submission made and mercy found.

Their stubborn neighbors who enraged,
United war against them waged,
By Joshua soon were overthrown,
For Gibeon's cause was now his own.

He, from whose arm they ruin feared,
Their leader and ally appeared
An emblem of the Savior's grace,
To those who humbly seek his face.

The men of Gibeon wore disguise,
And gained their peace by framing lies;
For Joshua had no pow'r to spare,
If he had known from whence they were.

But JESUS invitations sends,
Treating with rebels as his friends;
And holds the promise forth in view,
To all who for his mercy sue.

Too long his goodness I disdained,
Yet went at last and peace obtained;
But soon the noise of war I heard,
And former friends in arms appeared.

Weak in myself for help I cried,
LORD, I am pressed on every side;
The cause is thine, they fight with me,
But every blow is aimed at thee.

Olney Hymns
With speed to my relief he came,
And put my enemies to shame;
Thus saved by grace I live to sing,
The love and triumphs of my King.

JUDGES

Hymn 22
William Cowper
JEHOVAM-SHALEM,
The LORD send peace.
Judg 6:24

Jesus, whose blood so freely streamed
To satisfy the laws demand;
By thee from guilt and wrath redeemed,
Before the Father's face I stand.

To reconcile offending man,
Make Justice drop her angry rod;
What creature could have formed the plan,
Or who fulfil it but a God?

No drop remains of all the curse;
For wretches who deserved the whole;
No arrows dipped in wrath to pierce
The guilty, but returning soul.

Peace by such means co dearly bought,
What rebel could have hoped to see?
Peace, by his injured sovereign wrought,
His Sovereign fastened to the tree.

Now, LORD, thy feeble worm prepare!
For strife with earth and hell begins;
Confirm and gird me for the war,
They hate the soul that hates his sins.

Let them in horrid league agree!
They may assault, they may distress;
But cannot quench thy love to me,
Nor rob me of the LORD my peace.

Hymn 23
John Newton
GIDEON's fleece.
Judg 6:37-40

The signs which GOD to Gideon gave,
His holy Sovereignty made known;
That He alone has pow'r to save,
And claims the glory as his own.

The dew which first the fleece had filled,
When all the earth was dry around;
Was from it afterwards withheld,
And only fell upon the ground.

To Israel thus the heavenly dew
Of saving truth was long restrained;
Of which the Gentiles nothing knew,
But dry and desolate remained.

But now the Gentiles have received
The balmy dew of gospel peace
And Israel, who his spirit grieved,
Is left a dry and empty fleece.

This dew still falls at his command,
To keep his chosen plants alive;
They shall, though in a thirsty land,
Like willows by the waters thrive.
Is 44:4

But chiefly when his people meet,
To hear his word and seek his face;
The gentle dew, with influence sweet,
Descends and nourishes their grace.

But ah! what numbers still are dead,
Though under means of grace they lie!
The dew still falling round their head,
And yet their heart untouched and dry.

Dear Savior, hear us when we call,
To wrestling prayer an answer give;
Pour down thy dew upon us all,
That all may feel, and all may live.

Hymn 24
John Newton
SAMPSON's lion.
Judg 14:8

The lion that on Sampson roared,
And thirsted for his blood;
With honey afterwards was stored,
And furnished him with food.

Believers, as they pace along,
With many lions meet;
But gather sweetness from the strong,
And from the eater, meat.

The lions rage and roar in vain,
For Jesus is their shield;
Their losses prove a certain gain,
Their troubles comfort yield.

The world and Satan join their strength,
To fill their souls with fears;
But crops of joy they reap at length,
From what they sow in tears.

Afflictions make them love the word,
Stir up their hearts to prayer;
And many precious proofs afford,
Of their Redeemer's care.

The lions roar but cannot kill,
Then fear them not, my friends,
They bring us, though against their will,
The honey JESUS sends.

I SAMUEL

Hymn 25
John Newton
1Sam 1:10,18

When Hannah pressed with grief,
Poured forth her soul in prayer;
She quickly found relief,
And left her burden there:
Like her, in every trying case,
Let us approach the throne of grace.

When she began to pray,
Her heart was pained and sad;
But ere she went away,
Was comforted and glad:
In trouble, what a resting place,
Have they who know the throne of grace!

Though men and devils rage,
And threaten to devour;
The saints, from age to age,
Are safe from all their pow'r:
Fresh strength they gain to run their race,
By waiting at the throne of grace.

Eli her case mistook,
How was her spirit moved
By his unkind rebuke?
But GOD her cause approved.
We need not fear a creature's face,
While welcome at a throne of grace.

She was not filled with wine,
As Eli rashly thought;
But with a faith divine,
And found the help file sought:
Though men despise and call us base,
Still let us ply the throne of grace.

Men have not pow'r or skill,
With troubled souls to bear;
Though they express good-will,

John Newton

Poor comforters they are:
But swelling sorrows sink apace,
When we approach the throne of grace.

Numbers before have tried,
And found the promise true;
Nor one been yet denied,
Then why should I or you?
Let us by faith their footsteps trace,
And hasten to the throne of grace.

As fogs obscure the light,
And taint the morning air;
But soon are put to flight,
If the bright sun appear;
Thus Jesus will our troubles chase,
By shining from the throne of grace.[1]

Footnotes:
1. See also Book 2, Hymn 61

Hymn 26
John Newton
DAGON before the ark.
Judg 5:4,5

When first to make my heart his own,
The Lord revealed his mighty grace;
Self reigned, like Dagon, on the throne,
But could not long maintain its place.

It fell, and owned the pow'r divine,
(Grace can with ease the vict'ry gain)
But soon this wretched heart of mine,
Contrived to set it up again.

Again the LORD his name proclaimed,
And brought the hateful idol low;
Then self, like Dagon, broken, maimed,
Seemed to receive a mortal blow.

Yet self is not of life bereft,
Nor ceases to oppose his will;
Though but a maimed stump be left,
'Tis Dagon, 'tis an idol still.

Lord! must I always guilty prove,
And idols in my heart have room?
Hos 14:8
Oh! let the, fire of heavenly love,
The very slump of self consume.

Hymn 27
John Newton
The milch kine drawing the ark:
Faith's surrender of all
1Sam 6:12

The kine unguided went
By the directest road;
When the Philistines homeward sent
The ark of Israel's God.

Lowing they passed along,
And left their calves shut up;
They felt an instinct for their young,
But would not turn or stop.

Shall brutes, devoid of thought,
Their Maker's will obey;
And we, who by his grace are taught,
More stubborn prove than they?

He shed his precious blood
To make us his alone;
If washed in that atoning flood
We are no more our own.

If he his will reveal,
Let us obey his call;
And think whate'er the flesh may feel,
His love deserves our all.

We should maintain in view
His glory, as our end;
Too much we cannot bear, or do,
For such a matchless friend.

His saints should stand prepared
In duty's path to run;
Nor count their greatest trials hard,
So that his will be done.

With Jesus for our guide,
The path is safe though rough
The promise says, "I will provide,"
And faith replies, "Enough!"

Hymn 28
John Newton
SAUL's armor.
1Sam 17:38-40

When first my soul enlisted
My Savior's foes to fight;
Mistaken friends insisted
I was not armed aright:
So Saul advised David
He certainly would fail;
Nor could his life be saved
Without a coat of mail.

But David, though he yielded
To put the armor on,
Soon found he could not wield it,
And ventured forth with none.
With only sling and pebble
He fought the fight of faith;
The weapons seemed but feeble,
Yet proved Goliath's death.

Had I by him been guided,
And quickly thrown away
The armor men provided,
I might have gained the day;
But armed as they advised me,
My expectations failed;
My enemy surprised me,
And had almost prevailed.

Furnished with books and notions,
And arguments and pride
I practised all my motions,
And Satan's pow'r defied
But soon perceived with trouble,
That these would do no good;
Iron to him is stubble,
Job 41:27
And brass like rotten wood.

I triumphed at a distance
While he was out of sight;
But faint was my resistance

John Newton

When forced to join in fight:
He broke my sword in shivers,
And pierced my boasted shield;
Laughed at my vain endeavors,
And drove me from the field.

Satan will not be braved
By such a worm as I;
Then let me learn with David,
To trust in the Most High;
To plead the name of Jesus,
And use the sling of prayer;
Thus armed, when Satan sees us
He'll tremble and despair.

II SAMUEL

Hymn 29
John Newton
DAVID's fall
2Sam 11:27

How David, when by sin deceived,
From bad to worse went on!
For when the Holy Spirit's grieved,
Our strength and guard are gone.

His eye on Bathsheba once fixed,
With poison filled his soul;
He ventured on adult'ry next,
And murder crowned the whole.

So from a spark of fire at first,
That has not been descried;
A dreadful flame has often burst,
And ravaged far and wide.

When sin deceives it hardens too,
For though he vainly fought
To hide his crimes from public view,
Of God he little thought.

He neither would, or could repent,
No true compunction felt;
'Till God in mercy Nathan sent,
His stubborn heart to melt.

The parable held forth a fact,
Designed his case to show;
But though the picture was exact,
Himself he did not know.

"Thou art the man," the prophet said,
That word his slumber broke;
And when he owned his sin, and prayed,
The LORD forgiveness spoke.

John Newton

Let those who think they stand beware,
For David stood before;
Nor let the fallen soul despair,
For mercy can restore.

Hymn 30
John Newton
Is this thy kindness to thy friend.
2Sam 16:17

Poor, weak, and worthless though I am,
I have a rich almighty friend;
Jesus, the Savior, is his name,
He freely loves, and without end.

He ransomed me from hell with blood,
And by his pow'r my foes controlled;
He found me, wand'ring far from God,
And brought me to his chosen fold.

He cheers my heart, my wants supplies,
And says that I shall shortly be
Enthroned with him above the skies,
O! what a friend is CHRIST to me.

But ah! I my inmost spirit mourns,
And well my eyes with tears may swim,
To think of my perverse returns;
I've been a faithless friend to him.

Often my gracious Friend I grieve,
Neglect, distrust, and disobey,
And often Satan's lies believe,
Sooner than all my Friend can say.

He bids me always freely come,
And promises whate'er I ask:
But I am straitened, cold and dumb,
And count my privilege a task.

Before the world that hates his course,
My treach'rous heart has throbbed with shame;
Loth to forego the worlds applause,
I hardly dare avow his name.

Sure were not I most vile and base,
I could not thus my friend requite!
And were not he the God of grace,
He'd frown and spurn me from his sight.

I KINGS

Hymn 31
John Newton
Ask what I shall give thee.
1Ki 3:5

Come, my soul, thy suit prepare,
Jesus loves to answer prayer,
He himself has bid thee pray,
Therefore will not say thee nay.

Thou art coming to a King,
Ps 81:10
Large petitions with thee bring;
For his grace and pow'r are such,
None can ever ask too much.

With my burden I begin,
Lord, remove this load of sin!
Let thy blood, for sinners spilt,
Set my conscience free from guilt.

Lord! I come to thee for rest,
Take possession of my breast;
There thy blood-bought right maintain,
And without a rival reign.

As the image in the glass
Answers the beholder's face;
Thus unto my heart appear,
Print thine own resemblance there.

While I am a pilgrim here,
Let thy love my spirit cheer;
As my Guide, my Guard, my Friend,
Lead me to my journey's end.

Show me what I have to do,
Every hour my strength renew;
Let me live a life of faith,
Let me die thy peoples death.

Hymn 32
John Newton
Ask what I shall give thee.
1Ki 3:5

If Solomon for wisdom prayed,
The Lord before had made him wise;
Else he another choice had made,
And asked for what the worldlings prize.

Thus he invites his people still,
He first instructs them how to choose;
Then bids them ask whate'er they will,
Assured that He will not refuse.

Our wishes would our ruin prove,
Could we our wretched choice obtain;
Before we feel the Savior's love,
Kindle our love to him again.

But when our hearts perceive his worth,
Desires, till then unknown, take place;
Our spirits cleave no more to earth,
But pant for holiness and grace.

And dost thou say, "Ask what thou wilt?"
Lord, I would seize the golden hour;
I pray to be released from guilt,
And freed from sin and Satan's pow'r.

More of thy presence, Lord, impart,
More of thine image let me bear;
Erect thy throne within my heart,
And reign without a rival there.

Give me to read my pardon sealed,
And from thy joy to draw my strength;
To have thy boundless love revealed
In all its height, and breadth, and length.

Grant these requests, I ask no more
But to thy care the rest resign;
Sick or in health, or rich or poor,
All shall be well if thou art mine.

Hymn 33
John Newton
Ask what I shall give thee.
1Ki 3:5

Behold the throne of grace!
The promise calls me near;
There Jesus shows a smiling face,
And waits to answer prayer.

That rich atoning blood,
Which sprinkled round I see;
Provides for those who come to God,
An all-prevailing plea.

My soul ask what thou wilt,
Thou canst not be too bold;
Since his own blood for thee he spilt,
What else can he withhold.

Beyond thy utmost wants
His love and pow'r can bless;
To praying souls he always grants,
More than they can express.

Since 'tis the Lord's command,
My mouth I open wide;
Lord open thou thy bounteous hand,
That I may be supplied.

Thine image, LORD, bestow,
Thy presence and thy love;
I ask to serve thee here below,
And reign with thee above.

Teach me to live by faith,
Conform my will to thine;
Let me victorious be in death,
And then in glory shine.

If Thou these blessings give,
And wilt my portion be;
Cheerful the world's poor toys I leave,
To them who know not thee.

Hymn 34
John Newton
Queen of SHEBA
1Ki 10:1-9

From Sheba a distant report
Of Solomon's glory and fame,
Invited the queen to his court,
But all was outdone when she came;
She cried, with a pleasing surprise,
When first she before him appeared,
"How much, what I see with my eyes,
"Surpasses the rumor I heard!"

When once to Jerusalem come,
The treasure and train she had brought;
The wealth she possessed at home,
No longer had place in her thought:
His house, his attendants, his throne,
All struck her with wonder and awe;
The glory of Solomon shone,
In every object she saw.

But Solomon most she admired,
Whose spirit conducted the whole;
His wisdom, which God had inspired,
His bounty and greatness of soul;
Of all the hard questions she put,
A ready solution he showed;
Exceeded her with and her suit,
And more than she asked him bestowed.

Thus I when the gospel proclaimed
The Savior's great name in my ears,
The wisdom for which he is famed,
The love which to sinners he bears;
I longed, and I was not denied,
That I in his presence might bow;
I saw, and transported I cried,
"A greater than Solomon Thou!"

My conscience no comfort could find,
By doubt and hard questions opposed;
But He restored peace to my mind,
And answered each doubt I proposed:

John Newton

Beholding me poor and distressed,
His bounty supplied all my wants;
My prayer could have never expressed
So much as this Solomon grants.

I heard, and was slow to believe,
But now with my eyes I behold,
Much more than my heart could conceive,
Or language could ever have told:
How happy thy servants must be,
Who always before thee appear!
Vouchsafe, LORD, this blessing to me,
I find it is good to be here.

Hymn 35
John Newton
ELIJAH fed by ravens(s).
1Ki 17:6

Elijah's example declares,
Whatever distress may betide;
The saints may commit all their cares
To him who will surely provide:
When rain long withheld from the earth
Occasioned a famine of bread;
The prophet, secure from the dearth,
By ravens was constantly fed.

More likely to rob than to feed,
Were ravens who live upon prey;
But when the Lord's people have need,
His goodness will find out a way:
This instance to those may seem strange,
Who know not how faith can prevail;
But sooner all nature shall change,
Than one of God's promises fail.

Nor is it a singular case,
The wonder is often renewed;
And many can say, to his praise,
He sends them by ravens their food:
Thus worldlings, though ravens indeed,
Though greedy and selfish their mind,
If God has a servant to feed,
Against their own wills can be kind.[2]

Thus Satan, that raven unclean,
Who croaks in the ears of the saints;
Compelled by a power unseen,
Administers oft to their wants:
God teaches them how to find food
From all the temptations they feel;
This raven, who thirsts for my blood,
Has helped me to many a meal.

How safe and how happy are they
Who on the good Shepherd rely!
He gives them out strength for their day,
Their wants he will surely supply:

John Newton

He ravens and lions can tame,
All creatures obey his command;
Then let me rejoice in his name,
And leave all my cares in his hand.

Footnotes:
2. See also Book 3, Hymn 57

Hymn 36
John Newton
The meal and Cruse of oil.
1Ki 17:16

By the poor widow's oil and meal
Elijah was sustained;
Though small the stock it lasted well,
For God the store maintained.

It seemed as if from day to day,
They were to eat and die;
But still, though in a secret way,
He sent a fresh supply.

Thus to his poor he still will give
Just for the present hour;
But for tomorrow they must live
Upon his word and power.

No barn or storehouse they possess
On which they can depend;
Yet have no cause to fear distress,
For Jesus is their friend.

Then let not doubts your mind assail,
Remember, God has said,
"The cruse and barrel shall not fail,
"My people shall be fed."

And thus though faint it often seems,
He keeps their grace alive;
Supplied by his refreshing streams,
Their dying hopes revive.

Though in ourselves we have no stock,
The Lord is nigh to save;
His door flies open when we knock,
And 'tis but ask and have.

II KINGS

Hymn 37
John Newton
JERICHO; Or, The waters healed.
2Ki 2:19-22

Though Jericho pleasantly stood,
And looked like a promising soil;
The harvest produced little food,
To answer the husbandman's toil.
The water some property had,
Which poisonous proved to the ground;
The springs were corrupted and bad,
The streams spread a barrenness round.

But soon by the cruse and the salt,
Prepared by Elisha's command,
The water was cured of its fault,
And plenty enriched the land:
An emblem sure this of the grace
On fruitless dead sinners bestowed;
For man is in Jericho's case,
Till cured by the mercy of God.

How noble a creature he seems!
What knowledge, invention and skill!
How large and extensive his schemes!
How much can he do if he will!
His zeal to be learned and wise,
Will yield to no limits or bars;
He measures the earth and the skies,
And numbers and marshals the stars.

Yet still he is barren of good;
In vain are his talents and art;
For sin has infected his blood,
And poisoned the streams of his heart:
Though cockatrice eggs he can hatch,
Is 54:5
Or, spider-like, cobwebs can weave;
'Tis madness to labor and watch
For what will destroy or deceive.

Olney Hymns
But grace, like the salt in the cruse,
When cast in the spring of the soul;
A wonderful change will produce,
Diffusing new life through the whole:
The wilderness blooms like a rose,
The heart which was vile and abhorred;
Now fruitful and beautiful grows,
The garden and joy of the Lord.

Hymn 38
John Newton
NAAMAN.
2Ki 5:14

Before Elisha's gate
The Syrian leper stood;
But could not brook to wait,
He deemed himself too good:
He thought the prophet would attend,
And not to him a message send.

Have I this journey come,
And will he not be seen?
I were as well at home,
Would washing make me clean:
Why must I wash in Jordan's flood?
Damascus' rivers are as good.

Thus by his foolish pride
He almost missed a cure;
Howe'er at length he tried,
And found the method sure:
Soon as his pride was brought to yield,
The leprosy was quickly healed.

Leprous and proud as he,
To Jesus thus I came,
From sin to set me free,
When first I heard his fame:
Surely, thought I, my pompous train
Of vows and tears will notice gain.

My heart devised the way
Which I supposed he'd take;
And when I found delay,
Was ready to go back:
Had he some painful task enjoined,
I to performance seemed inclined.

When by his word he spake,
That fountain opened see;
'Twas opened for thy sake,
Go wash, and thou art free:"
O! how did my proud heart gainsay,

Olney Hymns
I feared to trust this simple way.

At length I trial made,
When I had much endured;
The message I obeyed,
I washed, and I was cured:
Sinners this healing fountain try,
Which cleansed a wretch so vile as I.

Hymn 39
John Newton
The borrowed axe.
2Ki 6:5,6

The prophets sons, in time of old,
Though to appearance poor;
Were rich without possessing gold,
And honored, though obscure.

In peace their daily bread they eat,
By honest labor earned;
While daily at Elisha's feet,
They grace and wisdom learned.

The prophet's presence cheered their toil,
They watched the words he spoke;
Whether they turned the furrowed soil,
Or felled the spreading oak.

Once as they listened to his theme,
Their conference was stopped;
For one beneath the yielding stream,
A borrowed axe had dropped.

"Alas! it was not mine, he said,
How shall I make it good?"
Elisha heard, and when he prayed,
The iron swam like wood.

If God, in such a small affair,
A miracle performs;
It shows his condescending care
Of poor unworthy worms.

Though kings and nations in his view
Are but as motes and dust;
His eye and ear are fixed on you,
Who in his mercy trust.

Not one concern of ours is small,
If we belong to him;
To teach us this, the LORD of all,
Once made the iron swim.

Hymn 40
John Newton
More with us than with them
2Ki 6:16

Alas! Elisha's servant cried,
When he the Syrian army spied,
But he was soon released from care,
In answer to the prophet's prayer.

Straitway he saw, with other eyes,
A greater army from the skies;
A fiery guard around the hill,
Thus are the saints preserved still.

When Satan and his host appear,
Like him of old, I faint and fear;
Like him, by faith, with joy I see,
A greater host engaged for me.

The saints espouse my cause by prayer,
The angels make my soul their care;
Mine is the promise sealed with blood,
And Jesus lives to make it good.

I CHRONICLES

Hymn 41
John Newton
Amazing Grace!
1Chr 17:16,17

Amazing grace! (how sweet the sound)
That saved a wretch like me!
I once was lost, but now am found,
Was blind, but now I see.

'Twas grace that taught my heart to fear,
And grace my fears relieved;
How precious did that grace appear,
The hour I first believed!

Through many dangers, toils and snares,
I have already come;
'Tis grace has brought me safe thus far,
And grace will lead me home.

The LORD has promised good to me,
His word my hope secures;
He will my shield and portion be,
As long as life endures.

Yes, when this flesh and heart shall fail,
And mortal life shall cease,
I shall possess, within the veil,
A life of joy and peace.

The earth shall soon dissolve like snow,
The sun forbear to shine;
But GOD, who called me here below,
Will be for ever mine.

NEHEMIAH

Hymn 42
John Newton
The joy of the Lord is your strength.
Neh 9:10

Joy is a fruit that will not grow
In nature's barren foil;
All we can boast, till CHRIST we know,
Is vanity and toil.

But where the LORD has planted grace;
And made his glories known;
There fruits of heavenly joy and peace
Are found, and there alone.

A bleeding Savior seen by faith,
A sense of pard'ning love;
A hope that triumphs over death,
Give joys like those above.

To take a glimpse within the veil,
To know that God is mine;
Are springs of joy that never fail,
Unspeakably divine!

These are the joys which satisfy,
And sanctify the mind;
Which make the spirit mount on high,
And leave the world behind.

No more, believers, mourn your lot,
But if you are the LORD'S;
Resign to them that know him not,
Such joys as earth affords.

JOB

Hymn 43
John Newton
Oh that I were as in months past!
Job 29:2

Sweet was the time when first I felt
The Savior's pard'ning blood
Applied, to cleanse my soul from guilt,
And bring me home to God.

Soon as the morn the light revealed,
His praises tuned my tongue;
And when the evening shades prevailed,
His love was all my song.

In vain the tempter spread his wiles,
The world no more could charm;
I lived upon my Savior's smiles,
And leaned upon his arm.

In prayer my soul drew near the Lord,
And saw his glory shine;
And when I read his holy word,
I called each promise mine.

Then to his saints I often spoke;
Of what his love had done;
But now my heart is almost broke,
For all my joys are gone.

Now when the evening shade prevails,
My soul in darkness mourns,
And when the morn the light reveals,
No light to me returns.

My prayers are now a chatt'ring noise,
For Jesus hides his face;
I read, the promise meets my eyes,
But will not reach my case.

Olney Hymns
Now Satan threatens to prevail,
And make my soul his prey;
Yet, Lord, thy mercies cannot fail,
O come without delay.

Hymn 44
John Newton
The change[3, 4]

Savior shine and cheer my soul,
Bid my dying hopes revive;
Make my wounded spirit whole,
Far away the tempter drive:
Speak the word and set me free,
Let me live alone to thee.

Shall I sigh and pray in vain,
Wilt thou still refuse to hear;
Wilt thou not return again,
Must I yield to black despair?
Thou hast taught my heart to pray,
Canst thou turn thy face away?

Once I thought my mountain strong,
Firmly fixed no more to move;
Then thy grace was all my song,
Then my soul was filled with love:
Those were happy golden days,
Sweetly spent in prayer and praise.

When my friends have said, "Beware,
Soon or late you'll find a change;"
I could see no cause for fear,
Vain their caution seemed and strange:
Not a cloud obscured my sky,
Could I think a tempest nigh?

Little, then, myself I knew,
Little thought of Satan's pow'r;
Now I find their words were true,
Now I feel the stormy hour!
Sin has put my joys to flight,
Sin has changed my day to night.

Satan asks, and mocks my woe,
"Boaster, where is now your God?"
Silence, Lord, this cruel foe,
Let him know I'm bought with blood:
Tell him, since I know thy name,
Though I change thou art the same.

Olney Hymns
Footnotes:
    3. See also Book 2, Hymn 34
    4. See also Book 3, Hymn 68

PSALMS

Hymn 45
John Newton
Pleading for mercy.
Ps 6

In mercy, not in wrath, rebuke
Thy feeble worm, my God!
My spirit dreads thine angry look,
And trembles at thy rod.

Have mercy, Lord, for I am weak,
Regard my heavy groans;
O let thy voice of comfort speak,
And heal my broken bones!

By day my busy beating head
Is filled with anxious fears;
By night, upon my restless bed,
I weep a flood of tears.

Thus I sit desolate and mourn,
Mine eyes grow dull with grief;
How long, my LORD, ere thou return,
And bring my soul relief?

O come and show thy pow'r to save,
And spare my fainting breath;
For who can praise thee in the grave,
Or sing thy name in death?

Satan, my cruel envious foe,
Insults me in my pain;
He smiles to see me brought so low,
And tells me hope is vain,

But hence, thou enemy, depart!
Nor tempt me to despair;
My Savior comes to cheer my heart,
The Lord has heard my prayer.

Hymn 46
John Newton
None upon earth I desire besides thee.
Ps 73:25

How tedious and tasteless the hours,
When JESUS no longer I see;
Sweet prospects, sweet birds, and sweet flow'rs,
Have lost all their sweetness with me:
The mid-summer sun shines but dim,
The fields strive in vain to look gay;
But when I am happy in Him,
December's as pleasant as May.

His name yields the richest perfume,
And sweeter than music his voice;
His presence disperses my gloom,
And makes all within me rejoice:
I should, were he always thus nigh,
Have nothing to wish or to fear;
No mortal so happy as I,
My summer would last all the year.

Content with beholding his face,
My all to his pleasure resigned;
No changes of season or place,
Would make any change in my mind:
While blessed with a sense of his love,
A palace a toy would appear;
And prisons would palaces prove,
If JESUS would dwell with me there.

Dear LORD, if indeed I am thine,
If thou art my sun and my song;
Say, why do I languish and pine,
And why are my winters so long?
O drive these dark clouds from my sky,
Thy soul-cheering presence restore;
Or take me unto thee on high,
Where winter and clouds are no more.

Hymn 47
John Newton
The believer's safety.
Ps 91

Incarnate God! the soul that knows
Thy name's mysterious power
Shall dwell in undisturbed repose,
Nor fear the trying hour.

Thy wisdom, faithfulness and love,
To feeble helpless worms;
A buckler and a refuge prove,
From enemies and storms.

In vain the fowler spreads his net,
To draw them from thy care;
Thy timely call instructs their feet,
To shun the artful snare.

When like a baneful pestilence,
Sin mows its thousands down
On every side, without defence,
Thy grace secures thine own.

No midnight terrors haunt their bed,
No arrow wounds by day;
Unhurt on serpents they shall tread,
If found in duty's way.

Angels, unseen, attend the saints,
And bear them in their arms;
To cheer the spirit when it faints,
And guard the life from harms.

The angels' Lord, himself is nigh,
To them that love his name;
Ready to save them when they cry,
And put their foes to shame.

Crosses and changes are their lot,
Long as they sojourn here;
But since their Savior changes not,
What have the saints to fear?

Hymn 48
John Newton
The believer's safety.
Ps 91

That man no guard or weapons needs,
Whose heart the blood of JESUS knows;
But safe may pass, if duty leads,
Through burning sands or mountain snows.

Released from guilt he feels no fear,
Redemption is his shield and tow'r;
He sees his Savior always near
To help, in every trying hour.

Though I am weak and Satan strong,
And often to assault me tries;
When Jesus is my shield and song,
Abashed the wolf before me flies.

His love possessing I am blest,
Secure whatever change may come;
Whether I go to East or West,
With him I still shall be at home.

If placed beneath the northern pole,
Though winter reigns with rigor there;
His gracious beams would cheer my soul,
And make a spring throughout the year.

Or if the deserts sun-burnt soil,
My lonely dwelling e'er should prove;
His presence would support my toil,
Whose smile is life, whose voice is love.

Hymn 49
John Newton
He led them by a right way.
Ps 107:7

When Israel was from Egypt freed,
The LORD, who brought them out,
Helped them in every time of need,
But led them round about.
Ex 13:17

To enter Canaan soon they hoped,
But quickly changed their mind;
When the Red Sea their passage stopped,
And Pharaoh marched behind.

The desert filled them with alarms,
For water and for food;
And Amalek, by force of arms,
To check their progress stood.

They often murmured by the way,
Because they judged by sight;
But were at length constrained to say,
The Lord had led them right.

In the Red Sea that stopped them first,
Their enemies were drowned;
The rocks gave water for their thirst,
And Manna spread the ground.

By fire and cloud their way was shown,
Across the pathless sands;
And Amalek was overthrown,
By Moses' lifted hands.

The way was right their hearts to prove,
To make GOD'S glory known;
And show his wisdom, pow'r and love,
Engaged to save his own.

Just so the true believer's path
Through many dangers lies;
Though dark to sense, 'tis right to faith,
And leads us to the skies.

Hymn 50
John Newton
What shall I render Ps 116:12,13[5]

For mercies, countless as the sands,
Which daily I receive
From Jesus, my Redeemer's hands,
My soul what canst thou give?

Alas! from such a heart as mine,
What can I bring him forth?
My best is stained and dyed with sin,
My all is nothing worth.

Yet this acknowledgment I'll make
For all he has bestowed;
Salvation's sacred cup I'll take
And call upon my God.

The best returns for one like me,
So wretched and so poor;
Is from his gifts to draw a plea,
And ask him still for more.

I cannot serve him as I ought,
No works have I to boast;
Yet would I glory in the thought
That I shall owe him most.

Footnotes:
5. See also Book 3, Hymn 67

John Newton

Hymn 51
John Newton
Dwelling in Mesech.
Ps 120:5-7

What a mournful life is mine,
Fill with crosses, pains and cares!
Every work defiled with sin,
Every step beset with snares!

If alone I pensive fit,
I myself can hardly bear;
If I pass along the street,
Sin and riot triumph there.

Jesus! how my heart is pained,
How it mourns for souls deceived!
When I hear thy name profaned,
When I see thy Spirit grieved!

When thy children's griefs I view,
Their distress becomes my own;
All I hear, or see, or do,
Makes me tremble, weep and groan.

Mourning thus I long had been,
When I heard my Savior's voice;
Thou hast cause to mourn for sin,
But in me thou may'st rejoice."

This kind word dispelled my grief,
Put to silence my complaints;
Though of sinners I am chief,
He his ranked me with his saints.

Though constrained to dwell a while
Where the wicked strive and brawl;
Let them frown; so he but smile,
Heav'n will make amends for all.

There, believers, we shall rest,
Free from sorrow, sin and fears;
Nothing there our peace molests,
Through eternal rounds of years.

Olney Hymns
Let us then the fight endure,
See our Captain looking down;
He will make the conquest sure,
And bestow the promised crown.

PROVERBS

Hymn 52
William Cowper
Wisdom.
Pr 8:22-31

Ere God had built the mountains,
Or raised the fruitful hills;
Before he filled the fountains
That feed the running rills;
In me, from everlasting,
The wonderful I AM,
Found pleasures never wasting,
And Wisdom is my name.

When, like a tent to dwell in,
He spread the skies abroad;
And swathed about the swelling
Of ocean's mighty flood;.
He wrought by weight and measure,
And I was with him then;
Myself the Father's pleasure,
And mine, the sons of men.

Thus wisdom's words discover
Thy glory and thy grace,
Thou everlasting lover
Of our unworthy race!
Thy gracious eye surveyed us
Ere stars were seen above.
In wisdom thou hast made us,
And died for us in love.

And couldst thou be delighted
With creatures such as we!
Who when we saw thee, slighted
And nailed thee to a tree?
Unfathomable wonder,
And mystery divine!
The voice that speaks in thunder,
Says, "Sinner I am thine!"

Hymn 53
John Newton
A friend that sticketh closer than a brother.
Pr 18:24

One there is, above all others,
Well deserves the name of friend;
His is love beyond a brother's,
Costly, free, and knows no end:
They who once his kindness prove,
Find it everlasting love!

Which of all our friends to save us,
Could or would have shed their blood?
But our JESUS died to have us
Reconciled, in him to God:
This was boundless love indeed!
JESUS is a friend in need.

Men, when raised to lofty stations,
Often know their friends no more;
Slight and scorn their poor relations
Though they valued them before.
But our Savior always owns
Those whom he redeemed with groans.

When he lived on earth abased,
Friend of sinners was his name;
Now, above all glory raised,
He rejoices in the same:
Still he calls them brethren, friends,
And to all their wants attends.

Could we bear from one another,
What he daily bears from us?
Yet this glorious Friend and Brother,
Loves us though we treat him thus:
Though for good we render ill,
He accounts us brethren still.

O for grace our hearts to soften!
Teach us, Lord, at length to love;
We, alas! forget too often,

John Newton

What a Friend we have above:
But when home our souls are brought,
We will love thee as we ought.

Hymn 54
John Newton
Vanity of Life[6]
Eccl 2

The evils that beset our path
Who can prevent or cure?
We stand upon the brink of death
When most we seem secure.

If we today sweet peace possess,
It soon may be withdrawn;
Some change may plunge us in distress,
Before tomorrow's dawn.

Disease and pain invade our health
And find an easy prey;
And oft, when least expected, wealth
Takes wings and flies away.

A fever or a blow can shake
Our wisdom's boasted rule;
And of the brightest genius make
A madman or a fool.

The gourds, from which we look for fruit,
Produce us only pain;
A worm unseen attacks the root,
And all our hopes are vain.

I pity those who seek no more
Than such a world can give;
Wretched they are, and blind, and poor,
And dying while they live.

Since sin has filled the earth with woe,
And creatures fade and die;
Lord wean our hearts from things below,
And fix our hopes on high.

Footnotes:
6. See also Book 2, Hymn 6

Hymn 55
William Cowper
Vanity of the world.

God gives his mercies to be spent;
"Your hoard will do your soul no good:
Gold is a blessing only lent,
Repaid by giving others food.

The world's esteem is but a bribe,
To buy their peace you fell your own;
The slave of a vain-glorious tribe,
Who hate you while they make you known.

The Joy that vain amusements give,
O! sad conclusion that it brings!
The honey of a crowded hive,
Defended by a thousand stings.

'Tis thus the world rewards the fools
That live upon her treach'rous smiles;
She leads them, blindfold, by her rules,
And ruins all whom she beguiles.

God knows the thousands who go down
From pleasure, into endless woe;
And with a long despairing groan
Blaspheme their Maker as they go.

O fearful thought! be timely wise;
Delight but in a Savior's charms;
And God shall take you to the skies,
Embraced in everlasting arms.

Hymn 56
John Newton
Vanity of the creature sanctified.

Honey though the bee prepares,
An envenomed sting he wears;
Piercing thorns a guard compose
Round the fragrant blooming rose.

Where we think to find a sweet,
Oft a painful sting we meet:
When the rose invites our eye,
We forget the thorn is nigh.

Why are thus our hopes beguiled?
Why are all our pleasures spoiled?
Why do agony and woe
From our choicest comforts grow?

Sin has been the cause of all!
'Twas not thus before the fall:
What but pain, and thorn, and sting,
From the root of sin can spring?

Now with every good we find
Vanity and grief entwined;
What we feel, or what we fear,
All our joys embitter here.

Yet, through the Redeemer's love,
These afflictions blessings prove;
He the wounding stings and thorns,
Into healing med'cines turns.

From the earth our hearts they wean,
Teach us on his arm to lean;
Urge us to a throne of grace,
Make us seek a resting place.

In the mansions of our King
Sweets abound without a sting;
Thornless there the roses blow,
And the joys unmingled flow.

SONG OF SOLOMON

Hymn 57
John Newton
The name of Jesus.
SS 1:3

How sweet the name of Jesus sounds
In a believer's ear?
It soothes his sorrows, heals his wounds,
And drives away his fear.

It makes the wounded spirit whole,
And calms the troubled breast;
'Tis Manna to the hungry soul,
And to the weary rest.

Dear name! the rock on which I build,
My shield and hiding place;
My never-failing treas'ry filled
With boundless stores of grace.

By thee my prayers acceptance gain,
Although with sin defiled,
Satan accuses me in vain,
And I am owned a child.

Jesus! my Shepherd, Husband, Friend,
My Prophet, Priest, and King;
My Lord, my Life, my Way, my End,
Accept the praise I bring.

Weak is the effort of my heart,
And cold my warmest thought;
But when I see thee as thou art,
I'll praise thee as I ought.

'Till then I would thy love proclaim
With every fleeting breath,
And may the music of thy name
Refresh my soul in death.

ISAIAH

Hymn 58
William Cowper
O LORD, I will praise thee!
Isa 12

I Will praise thee every day
Now thine anger's turned away!
Comfortable thoughts arise
From the bleeding sacrifice.

Here in the fair gospel field,
Wells of free salvation yield
Streams of life, a plenteous store,
And my soul shall thirst no more.

Jesus is become at length
My salvation and my strength;
And his praises shall prolong,
While I live, my pleasant song.

Praise ye, then, his glorious name,
Publish his exalted fame!
Still his worth your praise exceeds,
Excellent are all his deeds.

Raise again the joyful sound,
Let the nations roll it round!
Zion shout, for this is he,
God the Savior dwells in thee.

Hymn 59
John Newton
The Refuge, River, and Rock of the Church.
Isa 32:2

He who on earth as man was known,
And bore our sins and pains;
Now, seated on th' eternal throne,
The God of glory reigns.

His hands the wheels of nature guide
With an unerring skill;
And countless worlds extended wide,
Obey his sovereign will.

While harps unnumbered sound his praise,
In yonder world above;
His saints on earth admire his ways,
And glory in his love.

His righteousness, to faith revealed,
Wrought out for guilty worms,
Affords a hiding place and shield,
From enemies and storms.

This land, through which his pilgrims go,
Is desolate and dry;
But streams of grace from him o'erflow
Their thirst to satisfy.

When troubles, like a burning sun,
Beat heavy on their head;
To this almighty Rock they run,
And find a pleasing shade.

How glorious he! how happy they
In such a glorious friend!
Whose love secures them all the way,
And crowns them at the end.

Hymn 60
John Newton
Zion, or the city of God[7]
Isa 33:27,28

Glorious things of thee are spoken,
Ps 87:3
Zion, city of our God!
He, whose word cannot be broken,
Formed thee for his own abode:
Ps 132:14
On the rock of ages founded,
Mt 16:16
What can shake thy sure repose?
With salvation's walls surrounded
Isa 26:1
Thou may'st smile at all thy foes.

See! the streams of living waters
Springing from eternal love;
Ps 46:4
Well supply thy sons and daughters,
And all fear of want remove:
Who can faint while such a river
Ever flows their thirst t' assuage?
Grace, which like the LORD, the giver,
Never fails from age to age.

Round each habitation hov'ring
See the cloud and fire appear!
Isa 4:5,6
For a glory and a cov'ring,
Showing that the LORD is near:
Thus deriving from their banner
Light by night and shade by day;
Safe they feed upon the Manna
Which he gives them when they pray.

Blest inhabitants of Zion,
Washed in the Redeemer's blood!
Jesus, whom their souls rely on,
Makes them kings and priests to GOD:
Rev 1:6
'Tis his love his people raises
Over self to reign as kings

John Newton

And as priests, his solemn praises
Each for a thank-offering brings.

Savior, if of Zion's city
I through grace a member am;
Let the world deride or pity,
I will glory in thy name
Fading is the worldling's pleasure,
All his boasted pomp and show;
Solid joys and lasting treasure,
None but Zion's children know.

Footnotes:
7. See also Book 2, Hymn 24

Olney Hymns

Hymn 61
John Newton
Look unto me, and be ye saved.
Isa 45:22

As the serpent raised by Moses
Num 21:9
Healed the burning serpent's bite;
JESUS thus himself discloses
To the wounded sinner's sight:
Hear his gracious invitation,
"I have life and peace to give,
I have wrought out full salvation,
Sinner, look to me and live.

Pore upon your sins no longer,
Well I know their mighty guilt;
But my love than death is stronger,
I my blood have freely spilt:
Though your heart has long been hardened,
Look on me--it soft shall grow;
Past transgressions shall be pardoned,
And I'll wash you white as snow.

I have seen what you were doing,
Though you little thought of me;
You were madly bent on ruin,
But I said--It shall not be:
You had been for ever wretched,
Had I not espoused your part;
Now behold my arms outstretched
To receive you to my heart.

Well may shame, and joy, and wonder,
All your inward passions move;
I could crush thee with my thunder,
But I speak to thee in love:
See! your sins are all forgiven,
I have paid the countless sum!
Now my death has opened heaven,
Thither you shall shortly come."

Dearest Savior, we adore thee
For thy precious life and death;
Melt each stubborn heart before thee,

John Newton

Give us all the eye of faith:
From the law's condemning sentence,
To thy mercy we appeal;
Thou alone canst give repentance,
Thou alone our souls canst heal.

Hymn 62
John Newton
The good Physician.

How lost was my condition
Till JESUS made me whole!
There is but one Physician
Can cure a sin-sick soul.
Next door to death he found me,
And snatched me from the grave,
To tell to all around me,
His wondrous pow'r to save.

The worst of all diseases
Is light, compared with sin;
On every part it seizes,
But rages most within:
'Tis palsy, plague, and fever,
And madness--all combined;
And none but a believer
The least relief can find.

From men great skill professing
I thought a cure to gain;
But this proved more distressing,
And added to my pain:
Some said that nothing ailed me,
Some gave me up for lost;
Thus every refuge failed me,
And all my hopes were crossed.

At length this great Physician,
How matchless is his grace!
Accepted my petition,
And undertook my case:
First gave me sight to view him,
For sin my eyes had sealed;
Then bid me look unto him,
I looked, and I was healed.

A dying, risen Jesus,
Seen by the eye of faith;
At once from danger frees us,
And saves the soul from death:
Come then to this Physician,

John Newton

His help he'll freely give;
He makes no hard condition,
'Tis only--look and live.

Hymn 63
John Newton
To the afflicted, tossed with tempests and not comforted.
Isa 44:5-11

Pensive, doubting, fearful heart,
Hear what CHRIST the Savior says;
Every word should joy impart,
Change thy mourning into praise:
Yes, he speaks, and speaks to thee,
May he help thee to believe!
Then thou presently wilt see,
Thou hast little cause to grieve.

"Fear thou not, nor be ashamed,
All thy sorrows soon shall end
I who heav'n and earth have framed,
Am thy husband and thy friend
I the High and Holy One,
Israel's GOD by all adored;
As thy Savior will be known,
Thy Redeemer and thy Lord.

For a moment I withdrew,
And thy heart was filled with pain;
But my mercies I'll renew,
Thou shalt soon rejoice again:
Though I scorn to hide my face,
Very soon my wrath shall cease;
'Tis but for a moment's space,
Ending in eternal peace.

When my peaceful bow appears
Gen 9:13,14
Painted on the wat'ry cloud;
'Tis to dissipate thy fears,
Lest the earth should be o'erflowed:
'Tis an emblem too of grace,
Of my cov'nant love a sign;
Though the mountains leave their place,
Thou shalt be for ever mine.

Though afflicted, tempest-tossed,
Comfortless awhile thou art,
Do not think thou canst be lost,

John Newton

Thou art graven on my heart
All thy walls I will repair,
Thou shalt be rebuilt anew;
And in thee it shall appear,
What a God of love can do.

Hymn 64
William Cowper
The contrite heart.
Isa 47:15

The LORD will happiness divine
On contrite hearts bestow:
Then tell me, gracious GOD, is mine
A contrite heart, or no?

I hear, but seem to hear in vain,
Insensible as steel;
If ought is felt, 'tis only pain,
To find I cannot feel.

I sometimes think myself inclined
To love thee, if I could;
But often feel another mind,
Averse to all that's good.

My best desires are faint and few,
I fain would strive for more;
But when I cry, "My strength renew,"
Seem weaker than before.

Thy saints are comforted I know,
And love thy house of prayer;
I therefore go where others go,
But find no comfort there.

O make this heart rejoice, or ache;
Decide this doubt for me;
And if it be not broken, break,
And heal it, if it be.

Hymn 65
William Cowper
The future peace and glory of the church.
Isa 60:15-20

Hear what God the LORD hath spoken,
O my people, faint and few;
Comfortless, afflicted, broken,
Fair abodes I build for you:
Themes of heart-felt tribulation
Shall no more perplex your ways;
You shall name your walls, Salvation,
And your gates shall all be praise.

There, like streams that feed the garden,
Pleasures, without end, shall flow;
For the LORD, your faith rewarding,
All his bounty shall bestow:
Still in undisturbed possession,
Peace and righteousness shall reign;
Never shall you feel oppression,
Hear the voice of war again.

Ye no more your suns descending,
Waning moons no more shall see,
But your griefs, for ever ending,
Find eternal noon in me:
God shall rise, and shining o'er you,
Change to day the gloom of night;
He, the Lord, shall be your glory,
GOD your everlasting light.

JEREMIAH

Hymn 66
John Newton
Trust of the wicked, and the righteous compared.
Jer 17:5-8

As parched in the barren sands
Beneath a burning sky,
The worthless bramble with'ring stands,
And only grows to die.

Such is the sinner's aweful case,
Who makes the world his trust;
And dares his confidence to place
In vanity and dust.

A secret curse destroys his root,
And dries his moisture up;
He lives awhile, but bears no fruit,
Then dies without a hope.

But happy he whose hopes depend
Upon the LORD alone;
The soul that trusts in such a friend,
Can ne'er be overthrown.

Though gourds should wither, cisterns break,
And creature-comforts die;
No change his solid hope can shake,
Or stop his sure supply.

So thrives and blooms the tree whose roots
By constant streams are fed;
Arrayed in green, and rich in fruits,
It rears its branching head.

It thrives, though rain should be denied,
And drought around prevail;
'Tis planted by a river's side
Whose waters cannot fail.

Hymn 67
William Cowper
JEHOVAH our righteousness.
Jer 23:6

My God! how perfect are thy ways!
But mine polluted are;
Sin twines itself about my praise,
And slides into my prayer.

When I would speak what thou hast done
To save me from my sin;
I cannot make thy mercies known
But self-applause creeps in.

Divine desire, that holy flame
Thy grace creates in me;
Alas! impatience is its name,
When it returns to thee.

This heart, a fountain of vile thoughts,
How does it overflow?
While self upon the surface floats
Still bubbling from below.

Let others in the gaudy dress
Of fancied merit shine;
The LORD shall be my righteousness
The LORD for ever mine.

Hymn 68
William Cowper
EPHRAIM repenting.
Jer 31:18-20

My God! till I received thy stroke,
How like a beast was I!
So unaccustomed to the yoke,
So backward to comply.

With grief my just reproach I bear,
Shame fills me at the thought;
How frequent my rebellions were!
What wickedness I wrought!

Thy merciful restraint I scorned
And left the pleasant road;
Yet turn me, and I shall be turned,
Thou art the Lord my God.

Is Ephraim banished from my thoughts,
Or vile in my esteem?
No, saith the LORD, with all his faults,
I shall remember him.

Is he a dear and pleasant child?
Yes, dear and pleasant still;
Though sin his foolish heart beguiled,
And he withstood my will.

My sharp rebuke has laid him low,
He seeks my face again;
My pity kindles at his woe,
He shall not seek in vain.

LAMENTATIONS

Hymn 69
John Newton
The LORD is my portion.
Lam 3:24

From pole to pole let others roam,
And search in vain for bliss;
My soul is satisfied at home,
The Lord my portion is.

Jesus, who on his glorious throne
Rules heav'n and earth and sea;
Is pleased to claim me for his own,
And give himself to me.

His person fixes all my love,
His blood removes my fear;
And while he pleads for me above,
His arm preserves me here.

His word of promise is my food,
His Spirit is my guide;
Thus daily is my strength renewed
And all my wants supplied.[8]

For him I count as gain each loss,
Disgrace, for him, renown;
Well may I glory in his cross,
While he prepares my crown!

Let worldlings then indulge their boast,
How much they gain or spend!
Their joys must soon give up the ghost,
But mine shall know no end.

Footnotes:
    8. See also Book 3, Hymn 59

EZEKIEL

Hymn 70
John Newton
Humbled and silenced by mercy.
Ezek 16:64

Once perishing in blood I lay,
Creatures no help could give,
But Jesus passed me in the way,
He saw, and bid me live.

Though Satan still his rule maintained,
And all his arts employed;
That mighty Word his rage restrained,
I could not be destroyed.

At length the time of love arrived
When I my LORD should know,
Then Satan, of his pow'r deprived,
Was forced to let me go.

O can I e'er that day forget
When Jesus kindly spoke!
"Poor soul, my blood has paid thy debt,
And now I break thy yoke.

Henceforth I take thee for my own,
And give myself to thee;
Forsake the idols thou hast known,
And yield thyself to me."

Ah, worthless heart! it promised fair,
And said it would be thine;
I little thought it e'er would dare
Again with idols join.

LORD, dost thou such backslidings heal,
And pardon all that's past?
Sure, if I am not made of steel,
Thou hast prevailed at last.

John Newton

My tongue, which rashly spoke before,
This mercy will restrain;
Surely I now shall boast no more,
Nor censure, nor complain.

Hymn 71
William Cowper
The covenant.
Ezek 36:25-28

The Lord proclaims his grace abroad!
Behold, I change your hearts of stone;
Each shall renounce his idol god,
And serve, henceforth, the LORD alone.

My grace, a flowing stream, proceeds
To wash your filthiness away;
Ye shall abhor your former deeds,
And learn my statutes to obey.

My truth the great design insures,
I give myself away to you;
You shall be mine, I will be yours,
Your GOD unalterably true.

Yet not unsought, or unimplored,
The plenteous grace shall I confer;
Ezek 36:37
No--your whole hearts shall seek the Lord,
I'll put a praying spirit there.

From the first breath of life divine,
Down to the last expiring hour;
The gracious work shall all be mine,
Begun and ended in my pow'r.

John Newton

Hymn 72
William Cowper
JEHOVAH-SHAMMAH.
Ezek 48:33

As birds their infant brood protect,
Is 31:5
And spread their wings to shelter them;
Thus saith the LORD to his elect,
"So will I guard Jerusalem."

And what then is Jerusalem,
This darling object of his care?
Where is its worth in God's esteem,
Who built it? who inhabits there?

Jehovah founded it in blood,
The blood of his incarnate Son;
There dwell the saints, once foes to God,
The sinners, whom he calls his own.

There, though besieged on every side,
Yet much beloved and guarded well;
From age to age they have defied,
The utmost force of earth and hell.

Let earth repent, and hell despair,
This city has a sure defence;
Her name is called, the LORD is there,
And who has pow'r to drive him thence.

DANIEL

Hymn 73
John Newton
The power and triumph of faith.
Dan 3:6

Supported by the word,
Though in himself a worm,
The servant of the LORD
Can wondrous acts perform:
Without dismay he boldly treads
Where'er the path of duty leads.

The haughty king in vain,
With fury on his brow,
Believers would constrain
To golden gods to bow:
The furnace could not make them fear,
Because they knew the Lord was near.

As vain was the decree
Which charged them not to pray;
Daniel still bowed his knee,
And worshiped thrice a day:
Trusting in God, he feared not men,
Though threatened with the lion's den.

Secure they might refuse
Compliance with such laws,
For what had they to lose,
When GOD espoused their cause?
He made the hungry lions crouch,
Nor durst the fire his children touch.

The Lord is still the same,
A mighty shield and tow'r,
And they who trust his name
Are guarded by his pow'r:
He can the rage of lions tame,
And bear them harmless through the flame.

Yet we too often shrink
When trials are in view;

John Newton

Expecting we must sink,
And never can get through.
But could we once believe indeed,
From all these fears we should be freed.

Hymn 74
John Newton
BELSHAZZAR.
Dan 5:5,6

Poor sinners! little do they think
With whom they have to do!
But stand securely on the brink
Of everlasting woe.

Belshazzar thus, profanely bold,
The Lord of hosts defied;
But vengeance soon his boasts controlled,
And humbled all his pride.

He saw a hand upon the wall
(And trembled on his throne)
Which wrote his sudden dreadful fall
In characters unknown.

Why should he tremble at the view
Of what he could not read?
Foreboding conscience quickly knew
His ruin was decreed.

See him o'erwhelmed with deep distress!
His eyes with anguish roll;
His looks, and loosened joints, express
The terrors of his soul.

His pomp and music, guests and wine,
No more delight afford;
O sinner, ere this case be thine,
Begin to seek the LORD.

The law like this hand-writing stands,
And speaks the wrath of God;
Col 2:14
But JESUS answers its demands,
And cancels it with blood.

JONAH

Hymn 75
John Newton
The gourd.
Jonah 4:7

As once for Jonah, so the Lord
To soothe and cheer my mournful hours,
Prepared for me a pleasing gourd,
Cool was its shade, and sweet its flow'rs.

To prize his gift was surely right;
But through the folly of my heart,
It hid the Giver from my sight,
And soon my joy was changed to smart.

While I admired its beauteous form,
Its pleasant shade and graceful fruit;
The LORD, displeased, sent forth a worm,
Unseen, to prey upon the root.

I trembled when I saw it fade,
But guilt restrained the murm'ring word;
My folly I confessed, and prayed,
Forgive my sin, and spare my gourd.

His wondrous love can ne'er be told,
He heard me and relieved my pain;
His word the threat'ning worm controlled,
And bid my gourd revive again.

Now, Lord, my gourd is mine no more,
'Tis thine, who only couldst it raise;
The idol of my heart before,
Henceforth shall flourish to thy praise.

ZECHARIAH

Hymn 76
John Newton
Prayer for the Lord's promised presence.
Zech 2:10

Son of God! thy people's shield!
Must we still thine absence mourn?
Let thy promise be fulfilled,
Thou hast said, "I will return!"

Gracious Leader now appear,
Shine upon us with thy light!
Like the spring, when thou art near,
Days and suns are doubly bright.

As a mother counts the days
Till her absent son she see;
Longs and watches, weeps and prays,
So our spirits long for thee.

Come, and let us feel thee nigh,
Then thy sheep shall feed in peace;
Plenty bless us from on high,
Evil from amongst us cease.

With thy love, and voice, and aid,
Thou canst every care assuage;
Then we shall not be afraid,
Though the world and Satan rage.

Thus each day for thee we'll spend,
While our callings we pursue;
And the thoughts of such a friend
Shall each night our joy renew.

Let thy light be ne'er withdrawn,
Golden days afford us long!
Thus we pray at early dawn,
This shall be our evening song.

Hymn 77

John Newton
A brand plucked out of the fire.
Zech 3:1-5

With Satan, my accuser near,
My spirit trembled when I saw
The LORD in majesty appear,
And heard the language of his law.

In vain I wished and strove to hide
The tattered filthy rags I wore;
While my fierce foe, insulting cried,
"See what you trusted in before!"

Struck dumb, and left without a plea,
I heard my gracious Savior say,
"Know, Satan, I this sinner free,
I died to take his sins away.

This is a brand which I in love,
To save from wrath and sin design;
In vain thy accusations prove,
I answer all, and claim him mine."

At his rebuke the tempter fled;
Then he removed my filthy dress;
"Poor sinner take this robe, he said,
It is thy Savior's righteousness.

And see, a crown of life prepared!
That I might thus thy head adorn;
I thought no shame or suff'ring hard,
But wore, for thee, a crown of thorn."

O how I heard these gracious words!
They broke and healed my heart at once;
Constrained me to become the Lord's,
And all my idol-gods renounce.

Now, Satan, thou hast lost thy aim,
Against this brand thy threats are vain;
JESUS has plucked it from the flame,
And who shall put it in again?

Hymn 78
John Newton
On one stone shall be seven eyes.
Zech 3:9

Jesus Christ, the Lord's anointed,
Who his blood for sinners spilt;
Is the Stone by God appointed,
And the church is on him built:
He delivers all who trust him from their guilt.

Many eyes at once are fixed
On a person so divine;
Love, with aweful justice mixed,
In his great redemption shine:
Mighty JESUS! give me leave to call thee mine.

By the Father's eye approved,
Lo, a voice is heard from heav'n,
Mt 3:17
"Sinners, this is my Beloved,
For your ransom freely given:
All offences, for his sake, shall be forgiven."

Angels with their eyes pursued him,
1Tim 3:16
When he left his glorious throne;
With astonishment they viewed him
Put the form of servant on:
Angels worshipped him who was on earth unknown.

Satan and his host amazed,
Saw this stone in Zion laid;
Jesus, though to death abased,
Bruised the subtle serpent's head:
Jn 12:31
When to save us, on the cross his blood he shed.

When a guilty sinner sees him,
While he looks his soul is healed;
Soon this sight from anguish frees him,
And imparts a pardon sealed:
Jn 3:15
May this Savior be to all our hearts revealed!

John Newton

With desire and admiration,
All his blood-bought flock behold;
Him who wrought out their salvation,
And enclosed them in his fold:
1Pet 2:7
Yet their warmest love, and praises, are too cold.

By the eye of carnal reason
Many view him with disdain;
Ps 118:22
How will they abide the season
When he'll come with all his train:
To escape him then they'll wish, but wish in vain.

How their hearts will melt and tremble
When they hear his aweful voice;
Rev 1:7
But his saints he'll then assemble,
As his portion and his choice;
And receive them to his everlasting joys.

Hymn 79
William Cowper
Praise for the fountain opened.
Zech 13:1

There is a fountain filled with blood
Drawn from EMMANUEL'S veins;
And sinners, plunged beneath that flood,
Loose all their guilty stains.

The dying thief rejoiced to see
That fountain in his day;
And there have I, as vile as he,
Washed all my sins away.

Dear dying Lamb, thy precious blood
Shall never lose its pow'r;
Till all the ransomed church of God
Be saved, to sin no more.

E'er since, by faith, I saw the stream
Thy flowing wounds supply:
Redeeming love has been my theme,
And shall be till I die.

Then in a nobler sweeter song
I'll sing thy pow'r to save
When this poor lisping stamm'ring tongue
Lies silent in the grave.

Lord, I believe thou hast prepared
(Unworthy though I be)
For me a blood-bought free reward,
A golden harp for me!

'Tis strung, and tuned, for endless years,
And formed by pow'r divine;
To sound, in God the Father's ears,
No other name but thine.

MALACHI

Hymn 80
John Newton
They shall he mine, saith the Lord.
Mal 3:16-18

When sinners utter boasting words,
And glory in their shame;
The LORD, well-pleased, an ear affords
To those who fear his name.

They often meet to seek his face,
And what they do, or say,
Is noted in his book of grace
Against another day.

For they, by faith, a day descry,
And joyfully expect,
When he, descending from the sky,
His jewels will collect.

Unnoticed now, because unknown,
A poor and suff'ring few;
He comes to claim them for his own,
And bring them forth to view.

With transport then their Savior's care
And favor they shall prove;
As tender parents guard and spare
The children of their love.

Assembled worlds will then discern
The saints alone are blest;
When wrath shall like an oven burn,
And vengeance strike the rest.

MATTHEW

Hymn 81
John Newton
The beggar.
Mt 7:7-8

Encouraged by thy word
Of promise to the poor;
Behold, a beggar, LORD,
Waits at thy mercy's door!
No hand, no heart, O LORD, but thine,
Can help or pity wants like mine.

The beggar's usual plea
Relief from men to gain,
If offered unto thee,
I know thou would'st disdain:
And pleas which move thy gracious ear,
Are such as men would scorn to hear.

I have no right to say
That though I now am poor,
Yet once there was a day
When I possessed more:
Thou know'st that from my very birth,
I've been the poorest wretch on earth.

Nor can I dare profess,
As beggars often do,
Though great is my distress,
My wants have been but few:
If thou shouldst leave my soul to starve,
It would be what I well deserve.

'Twere folly to pretend
I never begged before;
Or if thou now befriend,
I'll trouble thee no more:
Thou often hast relieved my pain,
And often I must come again.

Though crumbs are much too good
For such a dog as I;

John Newton

No less than children's food
My soul can satisfy:
O do not frown and bid me go,
I must have all thou canst bestow.

Nor can I willing be
Thy bounty to conceal
From others, who like me,
Their wants and hunger feel:
I'll tell them of thy mercy's store,
And try to send a thousand more.

Thy thoughts, thou only wise!
Our thoughts and ways transcend,
Far as the arched skies
Above the earth extend:
Isa 45:8,9
Such pleas as mine men would not bear,
But God receives a beggar's prayer.

Hymn 82
John Newton
The leper.
Mt 8:23

Oft as the leper's case I read,
My own described I feel;
Sin is a leprosy indeed,
Which none but CHRIST can heal.

Awhile I would have passed for well,
And strove my spots to hide;
Till it broke out incurable,
Too plain to be denied.

Then from the saints I sought to flee,
And dreaded to be seen;
I thought they all would point at me,
And cry, "Unclean, unclean!"

What anguish did my soul endure,
Till hope and patience ceased?
The more I strove myself to cure,
The more the plague increased.

While thus I lay distressed, I saw
The Savior passing by;
To him, though filled with shame and awe,
I raised my mournful cry.

LORD, thou canst heal me if thou wilt,
For thou canst all things do;
O cleanse my leprous soul from guilt,
My filthy heart renew!

He heard, and with a gracious look,
Pronounced the healing word;
"I will, be clean" -- and while he spoke
I felt my health restored.

Come lepers, seize the present hour,
The Savior's grace to prove;
He can relieve, for he is pow'r,
He will, for he is love.

Hymn 83
John Newton
A sick soul
Mt 9:12

Physician of my sin-sick soul,
To thee I bring my case;
My raging malady control,
And heal me by thy grace.

Pity the anguish I endure,
See how I mourn and pine;
For never can I hope a cure
From any hand but thine.

I would disclose my whole complaint,
But where shall I begin?
No words of mine can fully paint
That worst distemper, sin.

It lies not in a single part,
But through my frame is spread;
A burning fever in my heart,
A palsy in my head.

It makes me deaf, and dumb, and blind,
And impotent and lame;
And overclouds, and fills my mind,
With folly, fear, and shame.

A thousand evil thoughts intrude
Tumultuous in my breast;
Which indispose me for my food,
And rob me of my rest.

Lord I am sick, regard my cry,
And set my spirit free;
Say, canst thou let a sinner die,
Who longs to live to thee?

Hymn 84
John Newton
Satan returning.
Mt 12:43-45

When Jesus claims the sinner's heart,
Where Satan ruled before;
The evil spirit must depart,
And dares return no more.

But when he goes without constraint,
And wanders from his home;
Although withdrawn, 'tis but a feint,
He means again to come.

Some outward change perhaps is seen
If Satan quit the place;
But though the house seem swept and clean,
'Tis destitute of grace.

Except the Savior dwell and reign
Within the sinner's mind;
Satan, when he returns again,
Will easy entrance find.

With rage and malice sevenfold,
He then resumes his sway;
No more by checks to be controlled,
No more to go away.

The sinner's former state was bad,
But worse the latter far;
He lives possessed, and blind, and mad,
And dies in dark despair.

Lord save me from this dreadful end!
And from this heart of mine,
O drive and keep away the fiend
Who fears no voice but thine.

Hymn 85
William Cowper
The sower.
Mt 13:3

Ye sons of earth prepare the plow,
Break up your fallow ground!
The Sower is gone forth to sow,
And scatter blessings round.

The seed that finds a stony soil,
Shoots forth a hasty blade;
But ill repays the sower's toil,
Soon withered, scorched, and dead.

The thorny ground is sure to baulk
All hopes of harvest there;
We find a tall and sickly stalk,
But not the fruitful ear.

The beaten path and highway side
Receive the trust in vain
The watchful birds the spoil divide,
And pick up all the grain.

But where the Lord of grace and pow'r
Has blessed the happy field;
How plenteous is the golden store
The deep-wrought furrows yield!

Father of mercies we have need
Of thy preparing grace;
Let the same hand that gives the seed,
Provide a fruitful place.

Hymn 86
John Newton
The wheat and tares.
Mt 13:37-42

Though in the outward church below
The wheat and tares together grow;
Jesus ere long will weed the crop,
And pluck the tares, in anger, up.

Will it relieve their horrors there,
To recollect their stations here?
How much they heard, how much they knew,
How long amongst the wheat they grew!

O! this will aggravate their case!
They perished under means of grace;
To them the word of life and faith,
Became an instrument of death.

We seem alike when thus we meet,
Strangers might think we all are wheat;
But to the Lord's all-searching eyes,
Each heart appears without disguise.

The tares are spared for various ends,
Some, for the sake of praying friends;
Others, the LORD, against their will,
Employs his counsels to fulfill.

But though they grow so tall and strong,
His plan will not require them long;
In harvest, when he saves his own,
The tares shall into hell be thrown.

Hymn 87
John Newton
Peter walking upon the water.
Mt 14:28-31

A Word from JESUS calms the sea,
The stormy wind controls;
And gives repose and liberty
To tempest-tossed souls.

To Peter on the waves he came,
And gave him instant peace;
Thus he to me revealed his name,
And bid my sorrows cease.

Then filled with wonder, joy and love,
Peter's request was mine;
LORD, call me down, I long to prove
That I am wholly thine.

Unmoved at all I have to meet
On life's tempestuous sea;
Hard, shall be easy; bitter, sweet,
So I may follow thee.

He heard and smiled, and bid me try,
I eagerly obeyed;
But when from him I turned my eye,
How was my soul dismayed!

The storm increased on every side,
I felt my spirit shrink;
And soon, with Peter, loud I cried,
LORD, save me, or I sink."

Kindly he caught me by the hand,
And said, "Why dost thou fear?
Since thou art come at my command,
And I am always near.

Upon my promise rest thy hope,
And keep my love in view;
I stand engaged to hold thee up,
And guide thee safely through."

Hymn 88
John Newton
Woman of Canaan.
Mt 15:22-28

Prayer an answer will obtain,
Though the Lord awhile delay;
None shall seek his face in vain,
None be empty sent away.

When the woman came from Tyre,
And for help to JESUS sought;
Though he granted her desire,
Yet at first he answered not.

Could she guess at his intent,
When he to his follow'rs said,
"I to Israel's sheep am sent,
Dogs must not have children's bread."

She was not of Israel's seed,
But of Canaan's wretched race;
Thought herself a dog indeed;
Was not this a hopeless case?

Yet although from Canaan sprung,
Though a dog herself she styled;
She had Israel's faith and tongue,
And was owned for Abraham's child.

From his words she draws a plea;
Though unworthy children's bread,
'Tis enough for one like me,
If with crumbs I may be fed.

Jesus then his heart revealed,
"Woman canst thou thus believe?
I to thy petition yield,
All that thou canst wish, receive.

'Tis a pattern set for us,
How we ought to wait and pray;
None who plead and wrestle thus,
Shall be empty sent away.

Hymn 89
John Newton
What think ye of Christ?
Mt 22:42

What think you of Christ? is the test
To try both your state and your scheme;
You cannot be right in the rest,
Unless you think rightly of him.
As Jesus appears in your view,
As he is beloved or not;
So God is disposed to you,
And mercy or wrath are your lot.

Some take him a creature to be,
A man, or an angel at most;
Sure these have not feelings like me,
Nor know themselves wretched and lost:
So guilty, so helpless, am I,
I durst not confide in his blood,
Nor on his protection rely,
Unless I were sure he is God.

Some call him a Savior, in word,
But mix their own works with his plan;
And hope he his help will afford,
When they have done all that they can:
If doings prove rather too light
(A little, they own, they may fail)
They purpose to make up full weight,
By casting his name in the scale.

Some style him the pearl of great price,
And say he's the fountain of joys;
Yet feed upon folly and vice,
And cleave to the world and its toys:
Like Judas, the Savior they kiss,
And, while they salute him, betray;
Ah! what will profession like this
Avail in his terrible day?

If asked what of JESUS I think?
Though still my best thoughts are but poor;
I say, he's my meat and my drink,
My life, and my strength, and my store,

Olney Hymns

My Shepherd, my Husband, my Friend,
My Savior from sin and from thrall;
My hope from beginning to end,
My Portion, my LORD, and my All.

Hymn 90
John Newton
7,6,7,6,7,7,7,6
The foolish virgins[9]
Mt 25:1

When descending from the sky
The Bridegroom shall appear;
And the solemn midnight cry,
Shall call professors near:
How the sound our hearts will damp!
How will shame o'erspread each face!
If we only have a lamp,
Without the oil of grace.

Foolish virgins then will wake
And seek for a supply;
But in vain the pains they take
To borrow or to buy:
Then with those they now despise,
Earnestly they'll wish to share;
But the best, among the wise,
Will have no oil to spare.

Wise are they, and truly blest,
Who then shall ready be
But despair will seize the rest,
And dreadful misery:
Once, they'll cry, we scorned to doubt,
Though in lies our trust we put;
Now our lamp of hope is out,
The door of mercy shut.

If they then presume to plead,
"Lord open to us now;
We on earth have heard and prayed,
And with thy saints did bow:"
He will answer from his throne,
"Though you with my people mixed,
Yet to me you ne'er were known,
Depart, your doom is fixed."

O that none who worship here
May hear that word, Depart!
LORD impress a godly fear

Olney Hymns
On each professor's heart:
Help us, Lord, to search the camp,
Let us not ourselves beguile;
Trusting to a dying lamp
Without a stock of oil.

Footnotes:
9. See also Book 3, Hymn 72

Hymn 91
John Newton
Peter sinning and repenting.
Mt 26:73

When Peter boasted, soon he fell,
Yet was by grace restored;
His case should be regarded well
By all who fear the Lord.

A voice it has, and helping hand,
Backsliders to recall;
And cautions those who think they stand,
Lest suddenly they fall.

He said, "Whatever others do,
With Jesus I'll abide;"
Yet soon amidst a murd'rous crew
His suff'ring Lord denied.

He who had been so bold before,
Now trembled like a leaf;
Not only lied, but cursed and swore,
To gain the more belief.

While he blasphemed he heard the cock,
And Jesus looked in love;
At once, as if by lightning struck,
His tongue forbore to move.

Delivered thus from Satan's snare
He starts, as from a sleep;
His Savior's look he could not bear,
But hasted forth to weep.

But sure the faithful cock had crowed
A hundred times in vain;
Had not the Lord that look bestowed,
The meaning to explain.

As I, like Peter, vows have made,
Yet acted Peter's part;
So conscience, like the cock, upbraids
My base, ungrateful heart.

Olney Hymns
Lord Jesus, hear a sinner's cry,
My broken peace renew;
And grant one pitying look, that I
May weep with Peter too.

MARK

Hymn 92
John Newton
The legion dispossessed.
Mk 5:18,19

Legion was my name by nature,
Satan raged within my breast;
Never misery was greater,
Never sinner more possessed:
Mischievous to all around me,
To myself the greatest foe;
Thus I was, when Jesus found me,
Filled with madness, sin and woe.

Yet in this forlorn condition,
When he came to see me free;
I replied, to my Physician,
"What have I to do with thee?"
But he would not be prevented,
Rescued me against my will;
Had he stayed till I consented,
I had been a captive still.

"Satan, though thou fain wouldst have it,
Know this soul is none of thine;
I have shed my blood to save it,
Now I challenge it for mine,[10]
Though it long has thee resembled,
Henceforth it shall me obey;"
Thus he spoke while Satan trembled,
Gnashed his teeth and fled away.

Thus my frantic soul he healed,
Bid my sins and sorrows cease;
"Take, said he, my pardon sealed,
I have saved thee, go in peace:"
Rather take me, LORD, to heaven,
Now thy love and grace I know;
Since thou hast my sins forgiven,
Why should I remain below?

"Love, he said, will sweeten labors,

Olney Hymns
Thou hast something yet to do;
Go and tell your friends and neighbors,
What my love has done for you:
Live to manifest my glory,
Wait for heav'n a little space;
Sinners, when they hear thy story,
Will repent and seek my face."

Footnotes:
10. See also Book 3, Hymn 54

Hymn 93
John Newton
The ruler's daughter raised.
Mk 5:39-42

Could the creatures help or ease us
Seldom should we think of prayer;
Few, if any, come to Jesus,
Till reduced to self-dispair:
Long we either slight or doubt him,
But when all the means we try,
Prove we cannot do without him,
Then at last to him we cry.

Thus the ruler when his daughter
Suffered much, though CHRIST was nigh,
Still deferred it, till he thought her
At the very point to die:
Though he mourned for her condition,
He did not entreat the Lord,
Till he found that no physician
But himself, could help afford.

Jesus did not once upbraid him,
That he had no sooner come;
But a gracious answer made him,
And went straitway with him home:
Yet his faith was put to trial
When his servants came, and said,
"Though he gave thee no denial,
'Tis too late, the child is dead."

Jesus; to prevent his grieving,
Kindly spoke and eased his pain;
"Be not fearful, but believing,
Thou shalt see her live again:"
When he found the people weeping,
"Cease, he said, no longer mourn;
For she is not dead, but sleeping,"
Then they laughed him to scorn.

O thou meek and lowly Savior,
How determined is thy love!
Not this rude unkind behavior,
Could thy gracious purpose move:

Olney Hymns
Soon as he the room had entered,
Spoke, and took her by the hand;
Death at once his prey surrendered,
And she lived at his command.

Fear not then, distressed believer,
Venture on his mighty name;
He is able to deliver,
And his love is still the same
Can his pity or his power,
Suffer thee to pray in vain;
Wait but his appointed hour,
And thy suit thou shalt obtain.

Hymn 94
John Newton
8,6,8,6
But one loaf[11]
Mk 8:14

When the disciples crossed the lake
With but one loaf on board;
How strangely did their hearts mistake
The caution of their Lord.

"The leaven of the Pharisees
Beware," the Savior said;
They thought, it is because he sees
We have forgotten bread.

It seems they had forgotten too,
What their own eyes had viewed;
How with what scarce sufficed for few,
He fed a multitude.

If five small loaves, by his command,
Could many thousands serve;
Might they not trust his gracious hand,
That they should never starve?

They oft his pow'r and love had known,
And doubtless were to blame;
But we have reason good to own
That we are just the same.

How often has he brought relief,
And every want supplied!
Yet soon, again, our unbelief
Says, "Can the Lord provide?"

Be thankful for one loaf today,
Though that be all your store;
Tomorrow, if you trust and pray,
Shall timely bring you more.

Footnotes:
11. See also Book 3, Hymn 57

Hymn 95
John Newton
BARTIMAEUS.
Mk 10:47,48

Mercy, O thou Son of David!
Thus blind Bartimaeus prayed;
Others by thy word are saved,
Now to me afford thine aid:
Many for his crying chid him,
But he called the louder still;
Till the gracious Savior bid him
"Come, and ask me what you will."

Money was not what he wanted,
Though by begging used to live;
But he asked, and JESUS granted
Alms, which none but he could give:
LORD remove this grievous blindness,
Let my eyes behold the day;
Strait he saw, and won by kindness,
Followed JESUS in the way.

O! methinks I hear him praising,
Publishing to all around;
"Friends, is not my case amazing?
What a Savior I have found:
O! that all the blind but knew him,
And would be advised by me!
Surely, would they hasten to him,
He would cause them all to see."

Hymn 96
William Cowper
The house of prayer.
Mk 11:17

Thy mansion is the christian's heart,
O LORD, thy dwelling-place secure!
Bid the unruly throng depart,
And leave the consecrated door.

Devoted as it is to thee,
A thievish swarm frequents the place;
They steal away my joys from me,
And rob my Savior of his praise.

There too a sharp designing trade
Sin, Satan, and the world, maintain;
Nor cease to press me, and persuade,
To part with ease and purchase pain.

I know them, and I hate their din,
Am weary of the bustling crowd;
But while their voice is heard within,
I cannot serve thee as I would.

O! for the joy thy presence gives,
What peace shall reign when thou art here!
Thy presence makes this den of thieves,
A calm delightful house of prayer.

And if thou make thy temple thine,
Yet, self-abased, will I adore;
The gold and silver are not mine,
I give thee what was thine before.

Hymn 97
John Newton
The blasted fig-tree.
Mk 11:20

One aweful word which JESUS spoke,
Against the tree which bore no fruit;
More piercing than the lightning's stroke,
Blasted and dried it to the root.

But could a tree the LORD offend,
To make him show his anger thus?
He surely had a farther end,
To be a warning word to us.

The fig-tree by its leaves was known,
But having not a fig to show;
It brought a heavy sentence down,
"Let none hereafter on thee grow."

Too many, who the gospel hear,
Whom Satan blinds and sin deceives;
We to this fig-tree may compare,
They yield no fruit, but only leaves.

Knowledge, and zeal, and gifts, and talk,
Unless combined with faith and love,
And witnessed by a gospel walk,
Will not a true profession prove.

Without the fruit the LORD expects
Knowledge will make our state the worse;.
The barren trees he still rejects,
And soon will blast them with his curse.

O LORD, unite our hearts in prayer!
On each of us thy Spirit send;
That we the fruits of grace may bear,
And find acceptance in the end.

LUKE

Hymn 98
John Newton
The two debtors.
Lk 7:47

Once a woman silent stood
While JESUS sat at meat;
From her eyes she poured a flood
To wash his sacred feet
Shame and wonder, joy and love;
All at once possessed her mind:
That she e'er so vile could prove,
Yet now forgiveness find.

"How came this vile woman here,
Will JESUS notice such?
Sure, if he a prophet were,
He would disdain her touch!"
Simon thus, with scornful heart,
Slighted one whom JESUS loved;
But her Savior took her part,
And thus his pride reproved.

"If two men in debt were bound,
One less, the other more;
Fifty, or five hundred pound,
And both alike were poor;
Should the lender both forgive,
When he saw them both distressed;
Which of them would you believe
Engaged to love him best?"

"Surely he who most did owe,"
The Pharisee replied;
Then our LORD, by judging so,
"Thou dost for her decide:
Simon if like her you knew
How much you forgiveness need;
You like her had acted too,
And welcomed me indeed!

Olney Hymns

When the load of sin is felt,
And much forgiveness known;
Then the heart of course will melt,
Though hard before as stone:
Blame not then her love and tears,
Greatly she in debt has been;
But I have removed her fears,
And pardoned all her sin."

When I read this woman's case,
Her love and humble zeal;
I confess, with shame of face,
My heart is made of steel,
Much has been forgiv'n to me,
JESUS paid my heavy score;
What a creature must I be
That I can love no more!

Hymn 99
John Newton
The good Samaritan.
Lk 10:33-35

How kind the good Samaritan
To him who fell among the thieves!
Thus Jesus pities fallen man,
And heals the wounds the soul receives.

O! I remember well the day,
When sorely wounded, nearly slain;
Like that poor man I bleeding lay,
And groaned for help, but groaned in vain.

Men saw me in this helpless case,
And passed without compassion by;
Each neighbor turned away his face,
Unmoved by my mournful cry.

But he whose name had been my scorn,
(As Jews Samaritans despise)
Came, when he saw me thus forlorn,
With love and pity in his eyes.

Gently he raised me from the ground,
Pressed me to lean upon his arm;
And into every gaping wound
He poured his own all-healing balm.

Unto his church my steps he led,
The house prepared for sinners lost;
Gave charge I should be clothed and fed;
And took upon him all the cost.

Thus saved from death, from want secured,
I wait till he again shall come,
(When I shall be completely cured)
And take me to his heav'nly home.

There through eternal boundless days,
When nature's wheel no longer rolls,
How shall I love, adore, and praise,
This good Samaritan to souls!

Hymn 100
John Newton
MARTHA and MARY.
Lk 10:38-42

Martha her love and joy expressed
By care to entertain her guest;
While Mary sat to hear her Lord,
And could not bear to lose a word.

The principle in both the same,
Produced in each a different aim;
The one to feast the LORD was led,
The other waited to be fed.

But Mary chose the better part,
Her Savior's words refreshed her heart;
While busy Martha angry grew,
And lost her time and temper too.

With warmth she to her sister spoke,
But brought upon herself rebuke;
One thing is needful, and but one,
Why do thy thoughts on many run?

How oft are we like Martha vexed,
Encumbered, hurried, and perplexed!
While trifles so engross our thought,
The one thing needful is forgot.

LORD teach us this one thing to choose,
Which they who gain can never lose;
Sufficient in itself alone,
And needful, were the world our own.

Let groveling hearts the world admire,
Thy love is all that I require!
Gladly I may the rest resign,
If the one needful thing be mine!

John Newton

Hymn 101
John Newton
The heart taken.
Lk 11:21,22

The castle of the human heart
Strong in its native sin;
Is guarded well, in every part,
By him who dwells within.

For Satan there, in arms, resides,
And calls the place his own;
With care against assaults provides,
And rules, as on a throne.

Each traitor thought on him, as chief,
In blind obedience waits;
And pride, self-will, and unbelief,
Are posted at the gates.

Thus Satan for a season reigns,
And keeps his goods in peace;
The soul is pleased to wear his chains,
Nor wishes a release.

But Jesus, stronger far than he,
In his appointed hour
Appears, to set his people free
From the usurper's pow'r.

"This heart I bought with blood, he says,
And now it shall be mine;"
His voice the strong one armed dismays,
He knows he must resign.

In spite of unbelief and pride,
And self, and Satan's art;
The gates of brass fly open wide,
And Jesus wins the heart.

The rebel soul that once withstood
The Savior's kindest call;
Rejoices now, by grace subdued,
To serve him with her all.

Hymn 102
John Newton
The worldling.
Lk 12:16-21

"My barns are full, my stores increase,
And now, for many years,
Soul, eat and drink, and take thine ease,
Secure from wants and fears."

Thus while a worldling boasted once,
As many now presume;
He heard the LORD himself pronounce
His sudden, aweful doom.

"This night, vain fool, thy soul must pass
Into a world unknown;
And who shall then the stores possess
Which thou hast called thine own."

Thus blinded mortals fondly scheme
For happiness below;
Till death disturb the pleasing dream,
And they awake to woe.

Ah! who can speak the vast dismay
That fills the sinner's mind;
When torn, by death's strong hand, away,
He leaves his all behind.

Wretches, who cleave to earthly things,
But are not rich to God;
Their dying hour is full of stings,
And hell their dark abode.

Dear Savior, make us timely wise,
Thy gospel to attend;
That we may live above the skies,
When this poor life shall end.

John Newton

Hymn 103
John Newton
The Barren fig-tree.
Lk 13:6-9

The church a garden is
In which believers stand,
Like ornamental trees
Planted by God's own hand:
His Spirit waters all their roots,
And every branch abounds with fruits.

But other trees there are,
In this enclosure grow;
Which, though they promise fair,
Have only leaves to show:
No fruits of grace are on them found,
They stand but cumb'rers of the ground.

The under gard'ner grieves,
In vain his strength he spends,
For heaps of useless leaves,
Afford him small amends:
He hears the LORD his will make known,
To cut the barren fig-trees down.

How difficult his post,
What pangs his bowels move,
To find his wishes crossed,
His labors useless prove!
His last relief is earnest prayer,
Lord, spare them yet another year.

Spare them, and let me try
What farther means may do;
I'll fresh manure apply,
My digging I'll renew
Who knows but yet they fruit may yield!
If not--'tis just, they must be felled.

If under means of grace,
No gracious fruits appear;
It is a dreadful case,
Though GOD may long forbear:
At length he'll strike the threatened blow,[12]

Olney Hymns
And lay the barren fig-tree low.

Footnotes:
12. See also Book 2, Hymn 26

Hymn 104
John Newton
The prodigal son.
Lk 15:11-24

Afflictions, though they seem severe;
In mercy oft are sent;
They stopped the prodigal's career,
And forced him to repent.

Although he no relentings felt
Till he had spent his store;
His stubborn heart began to melt
When famine pinched him sore.

"What have I gained by sin, he said,
But hunger, shame, and fear;
My father's house abounds with bread,
While I am starving here.

I'll go, and tell him all I've done,
And fall before his face
Unworthy to be called his son,
I'll seek a servant's place."

His father saw him coming back,
He saw, and ran, and smiled;
And threw his arms around the neck
Of his rebellious child.

"Father, I've sinned--but O forgive!"
I've heard enough, he said,
Rejoice my house, my son's alive,
For whom I mourned as dead.

Now let the fatted calf be slain,
And spread the news around;
My son was dead, but lives again,
Was lost, but now is found.

'Tis thus the Lord his love reveals,
To call poor sinners home;
More than a father's love he feels,
And welcomes all that come.

Hymn 105
John Newton
The rich man and LAZARUS.
Lk 16:19-25

A Worldling spent each day
In luxury and state;
While a believer lay,
A beggar at his gate:
Think not the LORD'S appointments strange,
Death made a great and lasting change.

Death brought the saint release
From want, disease, and scorn;
And to the land of peace,
His soul, by angels borne,
In Abraham's bosom safely placed,
Enjoys an everlasting feast.

The rich man also died,
And in a moment fell
From all his pomp and pride
Into the flames of hell:
The beggar's bliss from far beheld,
His soul with double anguish filled.

"O Abram send, he cries,
(But his request was vain)
The beggar from the skies
To mitigate my pain!
One drop of water I entreat,
To soothe my tongue's tormenting heat."

Let all who worldly pelf,
And worldly spirits have,
Observe, each for himself,
The answer Abram gave:
"Remember, thou wast filled with good,
While the poor beggar pined for food.

Neglected at thy door
With tears he begged his bread;
But now, he weeps no more,
His griefs and pains are fled:
His joys eternally will flow,

John Newton

While thine expire in endless woe."

LORD, make us truly wise,
To choose thy peoples' lot;
And earthly joys despise,
Which soon will be forgot:
The greatest evil we can fear,
Is to possess our portion here!

Hymn 106
John Newton
The importunate widow[13]
Lk 18:1-7

Our Lord, who knows full well
The heart of every saint;
Invites us, by a parable,
To pray and never faint.

He bows his gracious ear,
We never plead in vain;
Yet we must wait, till he appear,
And pray, and pray again.

Though unbelief suggest,
Why should we longer wait?
He bids us never give him rest,
But be importunate.

'Twas thus a widow poor,
Without support or friend,
Beset the unjust judge's door,
And gained, at last, her end.

For her he little cared,
As little for the laws;
Nor God, nor man, did he regard,
Yet he espoused her cause.

She urged him day and night,
Would no denial take;
At length he said, "I'll do her right,
For my own quiet sake."

And shall not Jesus hear
His chosen, when they cry?
Yes, though he may awhile forbear,
He'll help them from on high.

His nature, truth and love,
Engage him on their side;
When they are grieved, his bowels move,
And can they be denied?

John Newton

Then let us earnest be,
And never faint in prayer;
He loves our importunity,
And makes our cause his care.

Footnotes:
13. See also Book 2, Hymn 60

Olney Hymns

Hymn 107
John Newton
ZACCHEUS
Lk 19:1-6

Zaccheus climbed the tree,
And thought himself unknown;
But how surprised was he
When JESUS called him down!
The LORD beheld him, though concealed,
And by a word his pow'r revealed.

Wonder and joy at once
Were painted in his face;
Does he my name pronounce?
And does he know my case?
Will Jesus deign with me to dine?
Lord, I, with all I have, am thine!

Thus where the gospel's preached,
And sinners come to hear;
The hearts of some are reached
Before they are aware:
The word directly speaks to them,
And seems to point them out by name.

'Tis curiosity
Oft brings them in the way,
Only the man to see,
And hear what he can say;
But how the sinner starts to find
The preacher knows his inmost mind.

His long forgotten faults
Are brought again in view,
And all his secret thoughts
Revealed in public too:
Though compassed with a crowd about,
The searching word has found him out.

While thus distressing pain
And sorrow fills his heart,
He hears a voice again,

That bids his fears depart:
Then like Zaccheus he is blest,
And JESUS deigns to be his guest.

John Newton

Hymn 108
John Newton
The believer's danger, safety, and duty.
Lk 22:31,32

"Simon, beware! the Savior said,
Satan, your subtle foe,
Already has his measures laid
Your soul to overthrow.

He wants to sift you all, as wheat,
And thinks his vict'ry sure;
But I his malice will defeat,
My prayer shall faith secure."

Believers, tremble and rejoice,
Your help and danger view;
This warning has to you a voice,
This promise speaks to you.

Satan beholds, with jealous eye,
Your privilege and joy;
He's always watchful, always nigh,
To tear and to destroy.

But Jesus lives to intercede,
That faith may still prevail,
He will support in time of need,
And Satan's arts shall fail.

Yet, let us not the warning slight,
But watchful still be found;
Though faith cannot be slain in fight,
It may receive a wound.

While Satan watches, dare we sleep?
We must our guard maintain;
But, Lord, do thou the city keep,
Or else we watch in vain.
Ps 127:1

Hymn 109
John Newton
Father forgive them
Lk 23:34

"Father, forgive (the Savior said)
They know not what they do:"
His heart was moved when thus he prayed
For me, my friends, and you.

He saw, that as the Jews abused
And crucified his flesh;
So he, by us, would be refused,
And crucified afresh.

Through love of sin, we long were prone
To act as Satan bid;
But now, with grief and shame we own,
We knew not what we did.

We knew not the desert of sin,
Nor whom we thus defied;
Nor where our guilty souls had been,
If JESUS had not died.

We knew not what a law we broke,
How holy, just and pure!
Nor what a God we durst provoke,
But thought ourselves secure.

But Jesus all our guilt foresaw,
And shed his precious blood
To satisfy the holy law,
And make our peace with GOD.

My sin, dear Savior, made thee bleed,
Yet didst thou pray for me!
I knew not what I did, indeed,
When ignorant of thee.

Hymn 110
John Newton
The two malefactors.
Lk 23:39-43

Sovereign grace has pow'r alone
To subdue a heart of stone;
And the moment grace is felt,
Then the hardest heart will melt.

When the Lord was crucified,
Two transgressors with him died;
One with vile blaspheming tongue,
Scoffed at JESUS as he hung.

Thus he spent his wicked breath,
In the very jaws of death
Perished, as too many do,
With the Savior in his view.

But the other, touched with grace,
Saw the danger of his case;
Faith received to own the LORD,
Whom the scribes and priests abhorred.

"Lord, he prayed, remember me;
When in glory thou shalt be:"
"Soon with me, the Lord replies,
Thou shalt rest in paradise."

This was wondrous grace indeed,
Grace vouchsafed in time of need!
Sinners trust in Jesu's name,
You shall find him still the same.

But beware of unbelief,
Think upon the hardened thief;
If the gospel you disdain,
CHRIST, to you, will die in vain.

JOHN

Hymn 111
John Newton
The woman of Samaria.
Jn 4:28

Jesus, to what didst thou submit
To save thy dear-bought flock from hell!
Like a pour trav'ller see him sit,
Athirst, and weary, by the well.

The woman who for water came,
(What great events on small depend)
Then learnt the glory of his name,
The Well of life, the sinner's Friend!

Taught from her birth to hate the Jews,
And filled with party-pride; at first
Her zeal induced her to refuse
Water, to quench the Savior's thirst.

But soon she knew the gift of GOD,
And JESUS, whom she scorned before,
Unasked, that drink on her bestowed,
Which whoso tastes shall thirst no more.

His words her prejudice removed,
Her sin she felt, relief she found;
She saw and heard, believed and loved,
And ran to tell her neighbors round.

O come, this wondrous man behold!
The promised Savior! this is he,
Whom ancient prophecies foretold,
Born, from our guilt to set us free.

Like her, in ignorance content,
I worshipped long I knew not what;
Like her, on other things intent,
I found him, when I sought him not.

Olney Hymns
He told me all that e'er I did,
And told me all was pardoned too;
And now, like her, as he has bid,
I live to point him out to you.

Hymn 112

John Newton
The pool of Bethesda.[14]
Jn 5:2-4

Beside the gospel pool
Appointed for the poor;
From year to year, my helpless soul
Has waited for a cure.

How often have I seen
The healing waters move;
And others, round me, stepping in
Their efficacy prove.

But my complaints remain,
I feel the very same;
As full of guilt, and fear, and pain.
As when at first I came.

O would the LORD appear
My malady to heal;
He knows how long I've languished here;
And what distress I feel.

How often have I thought
Why should I longer lie?
Surely the mercy I have sought
Is not for such as I.

But whither can I go?
There is no other pool
Where streams of sovereign virtue flow
To make a sinner whole.

Here then, from day to day,
I'll wait, and hope, and try;
Can JESUS hear a sinner pray,
Yet suffer him to die?

No: he is full of grace;
He never will permit
A soul, that fain would see his face,
To perish at his feet.

Footnotes:
14. See also Book 3, Hymn 7

Hymn 113

John Newton
The pool of Bethesda. Jn 5:2-4[15]

Here at Bethesda's pool, the poor,
The withered, halt, and blind;
With waiting hearts expect a cure,
And free admittance find.

Here streams of wondrous virtue flow
To heal a sin-sick soul;
To wash the filthy white as snow,
And make the wounded whole.

The dumb break forth in songs of praise,
The blind their fight receive;
The cripple runs in wisdom's ways,
The dead revive, and live!

Restrained to no one case, or time,
These waters always move;
Sinners, in every age and clime,
Their vital influence prove.

Yet numbers daily near them lie,
Who meet with no relief;
With life in view they pine and die
In hopeless unbelief.

'Tis strange they should refuse to bathe,
And yet frequent the pool;
But none can even wish for faith,
While love of sin bears rule.

Satan their consciences has sealed,
And stupefied their thought;
For were they willing to be healed,
The cure would soon be wrought.

Do thou, dear Savior, interpose,
Their stubborn wills constrain;
Or else to them the water flows,
And grace is preached in vain.

Footnotes:
15. See also Book 3, Hymn 7

John Newton

Hymn 114
John Newton
The disciples at sea[16]
Jn 6:16-21

Constrained by their LORD to embark,
And venture, without him, to sea;
The season tempestuous and dark,
How grieved the disciples must be!
But though he remained on the shore,
He spent the night for them in prayer;
They still were as safe as before,
And equally under his care.

They strove, though in vain, for a while,
The force of the waves to withstand;
But when they were wearied with toil,
They saw their dear Savior at hand:
They gladly received him on board,
His presence their spirits revived;
The sea became calm at his word,
And soon at their port they arrived.

We, like the disciples, are tossed
By storms, on a perilous deep;
But cannot be possibly lost,
For Jesus has charge of the ship:
Though billows and winds are enraged,
And threaten to make us their sport;
This pilot his word has engaged
To bring us, in safety, to port.

If sometimes we struggle alone,
And he is withdrawn from our view;
It makes us more willing to own,
We nothing, without him, can do:
Then Satan our hopes would assail,
But JESUS is still within call;
And when our poor efforts quite fail,
He comes in good time and does all.

Yet, Lord, we are ready to shrink.
Unless we thy presence perceive;
O save us (we cry) or we sink,
We would, but we cannot believe

Olney Hymns
The night has been long and severe,
The winds and the seas are still high;
Dear Savior, this moment appear,
And say to our souls, "It is I!"[17]

Footnotes:
16. See also Book 2, Hymn 87
17. See also Book 3, Hymn 18

Hymn 115
John Newton
Will ye also go away?
Jn 6:67-69

When any turn from Zion's way,
(Alas! what numbers do!)
Methinks I hear my Savior say,
"Wilt thou forsake me too?"

Ah Lord! with such a heart as mine,
Unless thou hold me fast;
I feel I must, I shall decline,
And prove like them at last.

Yet thou alone hast pow'r, I know,
To save a wretch like me;
To whom, or whither, could I go,
If I should turn from thee?

Beyond a doubt I rest assured
Thou art the CHRIST of God;
Who hast eternal life secured
By promise and by blood.

The help of men and angels joined,
Could never reach my case;
Nor can I hope relief to find,
But in thy boundless grace.

No voice but thine can give me rest,
And bid my fears depart;
No love but thine can make me blest,
And satisfy my heart.

What anguish has that question stirred,
If I will also go?
Yet, LORD, relying on thy word,
I humbly answer, No!

Hymn 116
John Newton
The resurrection and the life.
Jn 11:25

"I Am, saith CHRIST our glorious head,
(May we attention give)
The resurrection of the dead,
The life of all that live.

By faith in me, the soul receives
New life, though dead before;
And he that in my name believes,
Shall live, to die no more.

The sinner, sleeping in his grave,
Shall at my voice awake;
And when I once begin to save,
My work I ne'er forsake."

Fulfill thy promise, gracious LORD,
On us assembled here,
Put forth thy Spirit with the word,
And cause the dead to hear.

Preserve the pow'r of faith alive,
In those who love thy name;
For sin and Satan daily strive
To quench the sacred flame.

Thy pow'r and mercy first prevailed
From death to set us free;
And often since our life had failed,
If not renewed by thee.

To thee we look, to thee we bow;
To thee, for help, we call;
Our life and resurrection thou,
Our hope, our joy, our all.

Hymn 117
John Newton
Weeping Mary
Jn 20:11-16

Mary to her Savior's tomb
Hasted at the early dawn;
Spice she brought, and sweet perfume,
But the LORD, The loved, was gone.
For awhile she weeping stood,
Struck with sorrow and surprise;
Shedding tears, a plenteous flood,
For her heart supplied her eyes.

Jesus, who is always near,
Though too often unperceived
Came, his drooping child to cheer,
And enquired, Why she grieved?
Though at first she knew him not,
When he called her by her name,
Then her griefs were all forgot,
For she found he was the same.

Grief and sighing quickly fled
When she heard his welcome voice;
Just before she thought him dead,
Now he bids her heart rejoice:
What a change his word can make,
Turning darkness into day!
You who weep for Jesus' sake;
He will wipe your tears away.

He who came to comfort her,
When she thought her all was lost;
Will for your relief appear,
Though you now are tempest-tossed:
On his word your burden cast,
On his love your thoughts employ;
Weeping for awhile may last,
But the morning brings the joy.

Hymn 118
William Cowper
Lovest thou me?
Jn 21:16

Hark, my soul! it is the LORD;
'Tis thy Savior, hear his word;
JESUS speaks, and speaks to thee;
"Say, poor sinner, lov'st thou me?

I delivered thee when bound,
And, when wounded, healed thy wound;
Sought thee wand'ring, set thee right,
Turned thy darkness into light."

Can a woman's tender care
Cease, towards the child she bare?
Yes, she may forgetful be,
Yet will I remember thee.

"Mine is an unchanging love;
Higher than the heights above;
Deeper than the depths beneath,
Free and faithful, strong as death.

Thou shalt see my glory soon,
When the work of grace is done;
Partner of my throne shalt be,
Say, poor sinner, lov'st thou me?"

Lord it is my chief complaint,
That my love is weak and faint;
Yet I love thee and adore,
Oh for grace to love thee more!

Hymn 119
John Newton
Lovest thou me?
Jn 21:16

'Tis a point I long to know,
Oft it causes anxious thought;
Do I love the LORD, or no?
Am I his, or am I not?

If I love, why am I thus?
Why this dull and lifeless frame?
Hardly, sure, can they be worse,
Who have never heard his name!

Could my heart so hard remain,
Prayer a task and burden prove;
Every trifle give me pain,
If I knew a Savior's love?

When I turn my eyes within,
All is dark, and vain, and wild;
Filled with unbelief and sin,
Can I deem myself a child?

If I pray, or hear, or read,
Sin is mixed with all I do;
You that love the LORD indeed,
Tell me, Is it thus with you?

Yet I mourn my stubborn will,
Find my sin, a grief, and thrall;
Should I grieve for what I feel,
If I did not love at all?

Could I joy his saints to meet,
Choose the ways I once abhorred,
Find, at times, the promise sweet,
If I did not love the LORD?

Lord decide the doubtful case!
Thou who art thy people's sun;
Shine upon thy work of grace,
If it be indeed begun.

Olney Hymns
Let me love thee more and more,
If I love at all, I pray;
If I have not loved before,
Help me to begin today.

ACTS

Hymn 120
John Newton
The death of STEPHEN.
Acts 7:54-60

As some tall rock amidst the waves,
The fury of the tempest braves;
While the fierce billows toiling high,
Break at its foot and murm'ring die:

Thus they, who in the LORD confide,
Though foes assault on every side;
Cannot be moved or overthrown,
For JESUS makes their cause his own.

So faithful Stephen, undismayed,
The malice of the Jews surveyed;
The holy joy which filled his breast
A lustre on his face impressed.

"Behold! he said, the world of light
Is opened to my strengthened sight;
My glorious LORD appears in view,
That JESUS, whom ye lately slew."

With such a friend and witness near,
No form of death could make him fear;
Calm, amidst show'rs of stones, he kneels,
And only for his murd'rers feels.

May we, by faith, perceive thee thus,
Dear Saviour, ever near to us!
This fight our peace, through life, shall keep,
And death be feared no more than sleep.

Hymn 121

John Newton
The rebel's surrender to grace.
Lord, what wilt thou have me to do?
Acts 9:6

Lord, thou hast won, at length I yield,
My heart, by mighty grace compelled,
Surrenders all to thee;
Against thy terrors long I strove,
But who can stand against thy love?
Love conquers even me.

All that a wretch could do, I tried,
Thy patience scorned, thy pow'r defied,
And trampled on thy laws;
Scarcely thy martyrs at the stake,
Could stand more steadfast for thy sake,
Than I in Satan's cause.

But since thou hast thy love revealed,
And shown my soul a pardon sealed,
I can resist no more:
Couldst thou for such a sinner bleed?
Canst thou for such a rebel plead?
I wonder and adore!

If thou hadst bid thy thunders roll,
And lightnings flash to blast my soul,
I still had stubborn been:
But mercy has my heart subdued,
A bleeding Savior I have viewed,
And now, I hate my sin.

Now, Lord, I would be thine alone,
Come take possession of thine own,
For thou hast set me free
Released from Satan's hard commands
See all my powers waiting stand,
To be employed by thee.

My will conformed to thine would move,
On thee my hope, desire, and love,
In fixed attention join;
My hands, my eyes, my ears, my tongue,

John Newton

Have Satan's servants been too long,
But now they shall be thine.

And can I be the very same,
Who lately durst blaspheme thy name;
And on thy gospel tread?
Surely each one, who hears my case,
Will praise thee, and confess thy grace
Invincible indeed!

Hymn 122
John Newton
PETER released from prison.
Acts 12:5-8

Fervent persevering prayers
Are faith's assured resource,
Brazen gates, and iron bars,
In vain withstand their force:
Peter when in prison cast,
Though by soldiers kept with care;
Though the doors were bolted fast,
Was soon released by prayer.

While he slept an angel came
And spread a light around;
Touched, and called him by his name,
And raised him from the ground:
All his chains and fetters burst,
Every door wide open flew;
Peter thought he dreamed, at first,
But found the vision true.

Thus the LORD can make a way
To bring his saints relief;
'Tis their part, to wait and pray,
In spite of unbelief:
He can break through walls of stone,
Sink the mountain to a plain;
They, to whom his name is known;
Can never pray in vain.

Thus in chains of guilt and sin,
Poor sinners sleeping lie;
No alarm is felt within,
Although condemned to die:
Till descending from above
(Mercy smiling in his eyes)
Jesus, with a voice of love,
Awakes, and bids them rise.

Glad the summons they obey,
And liberty desire;
Strait their fetters melt away,
Like wax before the fire:

John Newton

By the word of him who died,
Guilty pris'ners to release;
Every door flies open wide,
And they depart in peace.

Hymn 123
John Newton
The trembling jailer.
Acts 16:29,30

A Believer, free from care,
May in chains, or dungeons, sing,
If the Lord be with him there;
And he happier than a king:
Paul and Silas thus confined,
Though their backs were torn by whips,
Yet possessing peace of mind,
Sung his praise wish joyful lips.

Suddenly the prison shook,
Open flew the iron doors;
And the jailer, terror-struck,
Now his captives' help implores:
Trembling at their feet he fell,
"Tell me, Sirs, what must I do
To be saved from guilt and hell?
None can tell me this but you."

"Look to Jesus, they replied,
If on Him thou canst believe;
By the death which he has died,
Thou salvation shalt receive:"
While the living word he heard,
Faith sprung up within his heart;
And released from all he feared,
In their joy his soul had part.

Sinners, CHRIST is still the same,
O that you could likewise fear!
Then the mention of his name
Would be music to your ear:
JESUS rescues Satan's slaves,
His dear wounds still plead, "Forgive!"
JESUS to the utmost saves;
Sinners, look to him and live.

Hymn 124
John Newton
The exorcists.
Acts 19:13-16

Then the apostle wonders wrought,
And healed the sick, in Jesus' name;
The sons of Sceva vainly thought
That they had pow'r to do the fame.

On one possessed they tried their art,
And naming JESUS preached by Paul,
They charged the spirit to depart
Expecting he'd obey their call.

The spirit answered, with a mock,
"Jesus I know; and Paul I know;
I must have gone if Paul had spoke;
But who are ye that bid me go?"

With fury then the man he filled,
Who on the poor pretenders flew;
Naked and wounded, almost killed,
They fled in all the peoples' view.

Jesus! that name, pronounced by faith,
Is full of wonder-working pow'r;
It conquers Satan, sin and death,
And cheers in trouble's darkest hour.

But they, who are not born again,
Know nothing of it but the sound;
They do but take his name in vain
When most their zeal and pains abound.

Satan their vain attempts derides,
Whether they talk, or pray, or preach;
Long as the love of sin abides,
His pow'r is safe beyond their reach.

But you, believers, may rejoice,
Satan well knows your mighty Friend;
He trembles at your Savior's voice,
And owns he cannot gain his end.

Hymn 125
John Newton
PAUL's voyage.
Acts 27

If Paul in Caesar's court must stand,
He need not fear the sea;
Secured from harm, on every hand,
By the divine decree.

Although the ship, in which he sailed,
By dreadful storms was tossed;
The promise over all prevailed,
And not a life was lost.

Jesus! the GOD whom Paul adored,
Who saves in time of need;
Was then confessed, by all on board,
A present help indeed!

Though neither sun nor stars were seen
Paul knew the Lord was near;
And faith preserved his soul serene,
When others shook for fear.

Believers thus are tossed about
On life's tempestuous main;
But grace assures, beyond a doubt,
They shall their port attain.

They must, they shall appear one day,
Before their Savior's throne;
The storms they meet with by the way,
But make his power known.

Their passage lies across the brink
Of many a threat'ning wave;
The world expects to see them sink,
But JESUS lives to save.

Lord, though we are but feeble worms,
Yet since thy word is past;
We'll venture through a thousand storms,
To see thy face at last.

ROMANS

Hymn 126
John Newton
The good that I would I do not.
Rom 7

I would, but cannot sing,
Guilt has untuned my voice;
The serpent sin's envenomed sting
Has poisoned all my joys.

I know the Lord is nigh,
And would, but cannot, pray;
For Satan meets me when I try,
And frights my soul away.

I would but can't repent
Though I endeavor oft;
This stony heart can ne'er relent
Till JESUS make it soft.

I would but cannot love,
Though wooed by love divine;
No arguments have pow'r to move
A soul so base as mine.

I would, but cannot rest
In GOD'S most holy will;
I know what he appoints is best,
Yet murmur at it still!

Oh could I but believe!
Then all would easy be;
I would, but cannot, LORD relieve,
My help must come from thee!

But if indeed I would,
Though I can nothing do,
Yet the desire is something good,
For which my praise is due.

Olney Hymns
By nature prone to ill,
Till thine appointed hour
I was as destitute of will,
As now I am of pow'r.

Wilt thou not crown, at length,
The work thou hast begun?
And with a will, afford me strength
In all thy ways to run.

Hymn 127
John Newton
Salvation drawing nearer.
Rom 8

Darkness overspreads us here,
But the night wears fast away;
Jacob's star will soon appear,
Leading on eternal day!
Now 'tis time to rouse from sleep,
Trim our lamps and stand prepared;
For our LORD strict watch to keep,
Lest he find us off our guard.

Let his people courage take,
Bear with a submissive mind
All they suffer for his sake,
Rich amends they soon will find:
He will wipe away their tears,
Near himself appoint their lot;
All their sorrows, pains and fears,
Quickly then wilt be forgot.

Though already saved, by grace,
From the hour we first believed;
Yet while sin and war have place,
We have but a part received:
Still we for salvation wait,
Every hour it nearer comes!
Death will break the prison gate,
And admit us to our homes.

Sinners, what can you expect?
You who now the Savior dare;
Break his laws, his grace reject,
You must stand before his bar!
Tremble, lest he say, Depart!
Oh the horrors of that sound!
LORD, make every careless heart,
Seek thee while thou may'st be found.

I CORINTHIANS

Hymn 128
John Newton
That Rock was CHRIST.
1Cor 10:4

When Israel's tribes were parched with thirst,
Forth from the Rock the waters burst;
And all their future journey through,
Yielded them drink and gospel too!

In Moses' rod, a type they saw,
Of his severe and fiery law;
The smitten rock prefigured him,
From whose pierced side all blessings stream.

But ah! the types were all too faint,
His sorrows or his worth to paint;
Slight was the stroke of Moses' rod,
But he endured the wrath of God.

Their outward rock could feel no pain,
But ours was wounded, torn and slain;
The rock gave but a wat'ry flood,
But Jesus poured forth streams of blood.

The earth is like their wilderness,
A land of drought and sore distress;
Without one stream from pole to pole,
To satisfy a thirsty soul.

But let the Savior's praise resound!
In him refreshing streams are found;
Which pardon, strength, and comfort give,
And thirsty sinners drink and live.

II CORINTHIANS

Hymn 129
John Newton
My grace is sufficient for thee.
2Cor 12:9

Oppressed with unbelief and sin,
Fightings without, and fears within;
While earth and hell, with force combined,
Assault and terrify my mind.

What strength have I against such foes,
Such hosts and legions to oppose?
Alas! I tremble, faint, and fall,
LORD save me, or I give up all.

Thus sorely pressed I sought the LORD,
To give me some sweet cheering word;
Again I sought, and yet again,
I waited long, but not in vain.

O! 'twas a cheering word indeed!
Exactly suited to my need;
"Sufficient for thee is my grace,
Thy weakness my great pow'r displays."

Now despond and mourn no more,
I welcome all I feared before;
Though weak I'm strong, though troubled blest,
For CHRIST'S own pow'r shall on me rest.

My grace would soon exhausted be,
But his is boundless as the sea;
Then let me boast with holy Paul,
That I am nothing, CHRIST is all.

GALATIANS

Hymn 130
John Newton
The inward warfare.
Gal 5:17

Strange and mysterious is my life,
What opposites I feel within!
A stable peace, a constant strife,
The rule of grace, the pow'r of sin:
Too often I am captive led,
Yet daily triumph in my Head.

I prize the privilege of prayer,
But o! what backwardness to pray!
Though on the LORD I cast my care,
I feel its burden every day:
I seek his will in all I do,
Yet find my own is working too.

I call the promises my own,
And prize them more than mines of gold;
Yet though their sweetness I have known,
They leave me unimpressed and cold
One hour upon the truth I feed,
The next I know not what I read.

I love the holy day of rest,
When Jesus meets his gathered saints;
Sweet day, of all the week the best!
For its return my spirit pants:
Yet often, through my unbelief,
It proves a day of guilt and grief.

While on my Savior I rely,
I know my foes shall loose their aim;
And therefore dare their pow'r defy,
Assured of conquest through his name:
But soon my confidence is slain,
And all my fears return again.

John Newton

Thus different pow'rs within me strive,
And grace, and sin, by turns prevail;
I grieve, rejoice, decline, revive,
And vict'ry hangs in doubtful scale:
But JESUS has his promise passed,
That grace shall overcome at last.

PHILIPPIANS

Hymn 131
William Cowper
Contentment Php 4:11[18]

Fierce passions discompose the mind,
As tempests vex the sea;
But calm content and peace we find,
When, LORD, we turn to thee.

In vain by reason and by rule,
We try to bend the will;
For none, but in the Savior's school,
Can learn the heav'nly skill.

Since at his feet my soul has sat,
His gracious words to hear;
Contented with my present state,
I cast, on him, my care.

"Art thou a sinner, soul? he said,
Then how canst thou complain?
How light thy troubles here, if weighed
With everlasting pain!

If thou of murmuring wouldst be cured,
Compare thy griefs with mine;
Think what my love for thee endured,
And thou wilt not repine.

'Tis I appoint thy daily lot,
And I do all things well:
Thou soon shalt leave this wretched spot,
And rise with me to dwell.

In life my grace shall strength supply,
Proportioned to thy day;
At death thou still shalt find me nigh,
To wipe thy tears away."

John Newton

Thus I who once my wretched days,
In vain repinings spent;
Taught in my Savior's school of grace,
Have learned to be content.

Footnotes:
18. See also Book 3, Hymn 55

HEBREWS

Hymn 132
William Cowper
Old-Testament gospel
Heb 4:2

Israel in ancient days,
Not only had a view
Of Sinai in a blaze,
But learned the gospel too:
The types and figures were a glass
In which they saw the Savior's face.

The paschal sacrifice,
And blood-besprinkled door,
Ex 12:13
Seen with enlightened eyes,
And once applied with pow'r;
Would teach the need of other blood,
To reconcile an angry God.

The Lamb, the Dove, set forth
His perfect innocence,
Lev 12:6
Whose blood, of matchless worth,
Should be the soul's defence:
For he who can for sin atone,
Must have no failings of his own.

The scape-goat on his head
Lev 16:21
The peoples' trespass bore,
And to the desert led,
Was to be seen no more:
In him, our Surety seemed to say,
"Behold, I bear your sins away."

Dipped in his fellows' blood,
The living bird went free,
Lev 14:51-53
The type, well understood,
Expressed the sinner's plea;
Described a guilty soul enlarged,

John Newton

And by a Savior's death discharged.

Jesus I love to trace
Throughout the sacred page;
The footsteps of thy grace,
The same in every age!
O grant that I may faithful be
To clearer light, vouchsafed to me.

Hymn 133
John Newton
The word quick and powerful.
Heb 4:12,13

The word of CHRIST, our Lord,
With whom we have to do;
Is sharper than a two-edged sword,
To pierce the sinner through.

Swift as the lightnings blaze
When aweful thunders roll,
It fills the conscience with amaze,
And penetrates the soul.

No heart can he concealed
From his all-piercing eyes;
Each thought and purpose stands revealed,
Naked, without disguise.

He sees his peoples' fears,
He notes their mournful cry;
He counts their sighs and falling tears,
And helps them from on high.

Though feeble is their good,
It has his kind regard;
Yea, all they would do, if they could,
1Ki 8:18
Shall find a sure reward.

He sees the wicked too,
And will repay them soon,
For all the evil deeds they do,
And all they would have done.
Mt 5:28

Since all our secret ways
Are marked and known by thee;
Afford us, Lord, thy light of grace
That we ourselves may see.

Hymn 134
John Newton
Looking unto JESUS.
Heb 12:2

By various maxims, forms and rules,
That pass for wisdom in the schools,
I strove my passion to restrain;
But all my efforts proved in vain.

But since the Savior I have known
My rules are all reduced to one;
To keep my LORD, by faith, in view,
This strength supplies and motives too.

I see him lead a suff'ring life,
Patient, amidst reproach and strife;
And from his pattern courage take
To bear, and suffer, for his sake.

Upon the cross I see him bleed,
And by the sight from guilt am freed;
This sight destroys the life of sin,
And quickens heav'nly life within.

To look to Jesus as he rose
Confirms my faith, disarms my foes;
Satan I shame and overcome,
By pointing to my Savior's tomb.

Exalted on his glorious throne,
I see him make my cause his own;
Then all my anxious cares subside,
For Jesus lives, and will provide.

I see him look with pity down,
And hold in view the conqu'ror's crown;
If pressed with griefs and cares before,
My soul revives, nor asks for more.

By faith I see the hour at hand
When in his presence I shall stand;
Then it will be my endless bliss,
To see him where, and as he is.

Hymn 135
John Newton
Love-tokens.
Heb 12:5-11

Afflictions do not come alone,
A voice attends the rod;
By both he to his saints is known,
A Father and a GOD!

Let not my children slight the stroke
I for chastisement send;
Nor faint beneath my kind rebuke,
For still I am their friend.

The wicked I perhaps may leave
Awhile, and not reprove;
But all the children I receive
I scourge, because I love.

If therefore you were left without
This needful discipline;
You might, with cause, admit a doubt,
If you, indeed, were mine.

Shall earthly parents then expect
Their children to submit?
And wilt not you, when I correct,
Be humbled at my feet?

To please themselves they oft chastise,
And put their sons to pain;
But you are precious in my eyes,
And shall not smart in vain.

I see your hearts, at present, filled
With grief, and deep distress;
But soon these bitter seeds shall yield
The fruits of righteousness.

Break through the clouds, dear Lord, and shine!
Let us perceive thee nigh!
And to each mourning child of thine
These gracious words apply.

REVELATION

Hymn 136
John Newton
EPHESUS.
Rev 2:1,7

Thus saith the LORD to Ephesus,
And thus he speaks to some of us;
"Amidst my churches, lo, I stand,
And hold the pastors in my hand.

Thy works, to me, are fully known,
Thy patience, and thy toil, I own;
Thy views of gospel truth are clear,
Nor canst thou other doctrine bear.

Yet I must blame while I approve,
Where is thy first, thy fervent love?
Dost thou forget my love to thee,
That thine is grown so faint to me?

Recall to mind the happy days
When thou wast filled with joy and praise;
Repent, thy former works renew,
Then I'll restore thy comforts too.

Return at once, when I reprove,
Lest I thy candlestick remove;
And thou, too late, thy loss lament;
I warn before I strike, Repent."

Hearken to what the Spirit saith,
To him that overcomes by faith;
"The fruit of life's unfading tree,
In paradise his food shall be."

Hymn 137
John Newton
Smyrna.
Rev 2:11

The message first to Smyrna sent,
A message full of grace;
To all the Savior's flock is meant,
In every age and place.

Thus to his church, his chosen bride,
Saith the great First and Last;
"Who ever lives, though once he died,
Hold thy profession fast.

Thy works and sorrows well I know,.
Performed and borne for me;
Poor though thou art, despised and low,
Yet who is rich like thee?

I know thy foes, and what they say,
How long they have blasphemed;
The synagogue of Satan, they,
Though they would Jews be deemed.

Though Satan for a season rage,
And prisons be your lot;
I am your friend, and I engage
You shall not be forgot.

Be faithful unto death, nor fear
A few short days of strife;
Behold! the prize you soon shall wear,
A crown of endless life!"

Hear what the holy Spirit saith
Of all who overcome;
"They shall escape the second death,
The sinner's awful doom!"

John Newton

Hymn 138
William Cowper
Sardis.
Rev 3:1-6

"Write to Sardis, saith the Lord,
And write what He declares;
He whose Spirit, and whose word,
Upholds the seven stars:
All thy works and ways I search,
Find thy zeal and love decayed;
Thou art called a living church,
But thou art cold and dead.

Watch, remember, seek and strive,
Exert thy former pains;
Let thy timely care revive,
And strengthen what remains:
Cleanse thine heart, thy works amend:
Former times to mind recall;
Lest my sudden stroke descend,
And smite thee once for all.

Yet I number now, in thee,
A few that are upright;
These my Father's face shall see,
And walk with me in white:
When in judgment I appear,
They for mine shall be confessed;
Let my faithful servants hear,
And woe be to the rest.

Hymn 139
John Newton
Philadelphia
Rev 3:7-13

Thus saith the holy One, and true,
To his beloved faithful few;
"Of heav'n and hell I hold the keys,
To shut, or open, as I please.

I know thy works, and I approve,
Though small thy strength, sincere thy love;
Go on, my word and name to own,
For none shall rob thee of thy crown.

Before thee see my mercy's door
Stands open wide to shut no more;
Fear not temptation's fiery day,
For I will be thy strength and stay.

Thou hast my promise, hold it fast,
The trying hour will soon be past;
Rejoice, for lo! I quickly come,
To take thee to my heav'nly home.

A pillar there, no more to move,
Inscribed with all my names of love;
A monument of mighty grace,
Thou shalt for ever have a place."

Such is the conqueror's reward,
Prepared and promised by the Lord!
Let him that has the ear of faith,
Attend to what the Spirit saith.

Hymn 140
John Newton
Laodicea.
Rev 3:14-20

Hear what the Lord, the great Amen,
The true and faithful Witness says!
He formed the vast creation's plan,
And searches all our hearts and ways.

To some he speaks as once of old,
"I know thee, thy profession's vain;
Since thou art neither hot nor cold,
I'll spit thee from me with disdain.

Thou boasteth, "I am wise and rich,
Increased in goods and nothing need;"
And dost not know thou art a wretch,
Naked and poor, and blind and dead.

Yet while I thus rebuke, I love,
My message is in mercy sent;
That thou may'st my compassion prove,
I can forgive, if thou repent.

Wouldst thou be truly rich and wise?
Come, buy my gold in fire well tried,
My ointment to anoint thine eyes,
My robe, thy nakedness to hide.

See at thy door I stand and knock!
Poor sinner, shall I wait in vain?
Quickly thy stubborn heart unlock,
That I may enter with my train.

Thou canst not entertain a king,
Unworthy thou of such a guest!
But I my own provisions bring,
To make thy soul a heavenly feast."

Hymn 141
John Newton
The little book.[19]
Rev 10

When the beloved disciple took
The angels' little open book,
Which by the LORD'S command he eat,
It tasted bitter after sweet.

Thus when the gospel is embraced,
At first 'tis sweeter to the taste
Than honey, or the honey-comb,
But there's a bitterness to come.

What sweetness does the promise yield,
When by the Spirit's power sealed?
The longing soul is filled with good,
Nor feels a wish for other food.

By these inviting tastes allured,
We pass to what must be endured;
For soon we find it is decreed,
That bitter must to sweet succeed.

When sin revives and shows its pow'r.
When Satan threatens to devour,
When GOD afflicts and men revile,
We drag our steps with pain and toil.

When thus deserted, tempest-tossed,
The sense of former sweetness lost;
We tremble lest we were deceived
In thinking that we once believed.

The LORD first makes the sweetness known,
To win and fix us far his own;
And though we now some bitter meet,
We hope for everlasting sweet.

Footnotes:
19. See also Book 3, Hymn 27

BOOK II
On Occasional Subjects.
  1. SEASONS.
  2. ORDINANCES
  3. PROVIDENCES.
  4. CREATION.

I. SEASONS
NEW-YEAR'S HYMNS.

Hymn 1
John Newton
Time how swift.

While with ceaseless course the sun
Hasted through the former year,
Many souls their race have run,
Never more to meet us here
Fixed in an eternal fate,
They have done with all below;
We a little longer wait,
But how little--none can know.

As the winged arrow flies
Speedily the mark to find;
As the lightning from the skies
Darts, and leaves no trace behind;
Swiftly thus our fleeting days
Bear us down life's rapid stream;
Upwards, Lord, our spirits raise,
All below is but a dream.

Thanks for mercies past receive,
Pardon of our sins renew;
Teach us, henceforth, how to live
With eternity in view:
Bless thy word to young and old,
Fill us with a Savior's love;
And when life's short tale is told,
May we dwell with thee above.

Hymn 2
John Newton
Time how short.

Time, with an unwearied hand,
Pushes round the seasons past,
And in life's frail glass, the sand
Sinks apace, not long to last:
Many, well as you or I,
Who last year assembled thus;
In their silent graves now lie,
Graves will open soon for us!

Daily sin, and care, and strife,
While the Lord prolongs our breath,
Make it but a dying life,
Or a kind of living death:
Wretched they, and most forlorn,
Who no better portion know;
Better ne'er to have been born,
Than to have our all below.

When constrained to go alone,
Leaving all you love behind;
Ent'ring on a world unknown,
What will then support your mind?
When the Lord his summons sends,
Is 10:3
Earthly comforts lose their pow'r;
Honors, riches, kindred, friends,
Cannot cheer a dying hour.

Happy souls who fear the LORD
Time is not too swift for you;
When your Savior gives the word,
Glad you'll bid the world adieu:
Then he'll wipe away your tears,
Near himself appoint your place;
Swifter fly, ye rolling years,
LORD, we long to see thy face.

Hymn 3
John Newton
Uncertainty of life.

See! another year is gone!
Quickly have the seasons past!
This we enter now upon
May to many prove our last.
Mercy hitherto has spared,
But have mercies been improved?
Let us ask, am I prepared
Should I be this year removed?

Some we now no longer see,
Who their mortal race have run;
Seemed as fair for life as we,
When the former year begun
Some, but who God only knows,
Who are here assembled now;
Ere the present year shall close,
To the stroke of death must bow.

Life a field of battle is,
Thousands fall within our view;
And the next death-bolt that flies,
May be sent to me or you:
While we preach, and while we hear,
Help us, LORD, each one, to think,
Vast eternity is near,
I am standing on the brink.

If from guilt and sin set free,
By the knowledge of thy grace;
Welcome, then, the call will be
To depart and see thy face:
To thy saints, while here below,
With new years, new mercies come;
But the happiest year they know
Is their last, which leads them home.

Hymn 4
John Newton
A new-year's thought and prayer.

Time, by moments, steals away,
First the hour, and then the day;
Small the daily loss appears,
Yet it soon amounts to years:
Thus another year is flown,
Now it is no more our own
(If it brought or promised good)
Than the years before the flood.

But (may none of us forget)
It has left us much in debt;
Favors from the LORD received,
Sins that have his Spirit grieved;
Marked by an unerring hand
In his book recorded stand;
Who can tell the vast amount,
Placed to each of our account?

Happy, the believing soul!
CHRIST for you has paid the whole;
While you own the debt is large,
You may plead a full discharge:
But poor careless sinner, say,
What can you to justice pay?
Tremble, lest when life is past,
Into prison you be cast!

Will you still increase the score?
Still be careless, as before?
O, forbid it, gracious Lord,
Touch their spirits by thy word!
Now, in mercy, to them show
What a mighty debt they owe!
All their unbelief subdue,
Let them find forgiveness too.

Spared to see another year,
Let thy blessing meet us here;
Come, thy dying work revive,

John Newton

Bid thy drooping garden thrive:
Sun of righteousness arise!
Warm our hearts, and bless our eyes;
Let our prayer thy bowels move,
Make this year a time of love!

Olney Hymns

Hymn 5
John Newton
Death and war. 1778.

Hark! how time's wide sounding bell
Strikes on each attentive ear!
Tolling loud the solemn knell
Of the late departed year:
Years, like mortals, wear away,
Have their birth, and dying day;
Youthful spring, and wintry age,
Then to others quit the stage.

Sad experience may relate
What a year the last has been!
Crops of sorrow have been great,
From the fruitful seeds of sin:
O! what numbers gay and blithe,
Fell by death's unsparing scythe?
While they thought the world their own,
Suddenly he mowed them down.

See how war, with dreadful stride,
Marches at the LORD'S command,
Spreading desolation wide,
Through a once much-favored land:
War, with heart and arms of steel,
Preys on thousands at a meal;
Daily drinking human gore,
Still he thirsts, and calls for more.

If the God, whom we provoke,
Hither should his way direct;
What a sin-avenging stroke
May a land, like this, expect!
They who now securely sleep,
Quickly then, would wake and weep;
And too late would learn to fear,
When they saw the danger near.

You are safe, who know his love,
He will all his truth perform;
To your souls a refuge prove

John Newton

From the rage of every storm:
But we tremble for the youth;
Teach them, Lord, thy saving truth;
Join them to thy faithful few,
Be to them a refuge too.

Hymn 6
John Newton
Earthly prospects deceitful.

Oft in vain the voice of truth,
Solemnly and loudly warns;
Thoughtless, inexperienced youth,
Though it hears, the warning scorns:
Youth in fancy's glass surveys
Life prolonged to distant years;
While the vast, imagined space,
Filled with sweets and joys appears.

Aweful disappointment, soon
Overclouds the prospect gay!
Some their sun goes down at noon,
Torn by death's strong hand away:
Where are then their pleasing schemes?
Where the joys they hoped to find?
Gone for ever, like their dreams,
Leaving not a trace behind.

Others, who are spared awhile,
Live to weep o'er fancy's cheat;
Find distress, and pain, and toil,
Bitter things instead of sweet:
Sin has spread a curse around,
Poisoned all things here below;
On this base polluted ground,
Peace and joy can never grow.

Grace alone can cure our ills,
Sweeten life, with all its cares;
Regulate our stubborn wills,
Save us from surrounding snares
Though you oft have heard in vain,
Former years in folly spent;
Grace invites you yet again,
Once more calls you to repent.

Called again, at length, beware,
Hear the Savior's voice, and live;
Lest he in his wrath should swear,

John Newton

He no more will warning give:
Pray, that you may hear and feel,
Ere the day of grace be past;
Lest your hearts grow hard as steel,
Or this year should prove your last.

HYMNS before annual Sermons to young people, on new-years evenings.

Hymn 7
John Newton
Prayer for a blessing.

Now, gracious Lord, thine arm reveal,
And wake thy glory known;
Now let us all thy presence feel,
And soften hearts of stone!

Help us to venture near thy throne,
And plead a Savior's name;
For all that we can call our own,
Is vanity and shame.

From all the guilt of former sin
May mercy set us free;
And let the year we now begin,
Begin and end with thee.

Send down thy Spirit from above
That saints may love thee more;
And sinners now may learn to love
Who never loved before.

And when before thee we appear
In our eternal home;
May growing numbers worship here,
And praise thee in our room.

John Newton

Hymn 8
William Cowper
Prayer for a blessing.

Bestow, dear Lord, upon our youth
The gift of saving grace;
And let the seed of sacred truth
Fall in a fruitful place.

Grace is a plant, where'er it grows,
Of pure and heav'nly root;
But fairest in the youngest shows,
And yields the sweetest fruit;

Ye careless ones, O hear betimes
The voice of sovereign love!
Your youth is stained with many crimes,
But mercy reigns above.

True, you are young, but there's a stone
Within the youngest breast;
Or half the crimes which you have done.
Would rob you of your rest.

For you the public prayer is made,
O! join the public prayer!
For you the secret tear is shed,
O shed yourselves a tear.

We pray that you may early prove
The Spirit's power to teach;
You cannot be too young to love
That JESUS whom we preach.

Hymn 9
John Newton
Prayer for a blessing.

Now may fervent prayer arise
Winged with faith, and pierce the skies;
Fervent prayer shall bring us down
Gracious answers from the throne.

Bless, O LORD, the op'ning year
To each soul assembled here;
Clothe thy word with pow'r divine,
Make us willing to be thine.

Shepherd of thy blood-bought sheep!
Teach the stony heart to weep;
Let the blind have eyes to see,
See themselves, and look on thee!

Let the minds of all our youth
Feel the force of sacred truth;
While the gospel-call they hear
May they learn to love and fear!

Show them what their ways have been,
Show them the desert of sin;
Then thy dying love reveal,
This shall melt a heart of steel.

Where thou hast thy work begun,
Give new strength the race to run;
Scatter darkness, doubts and fears,
Wipe away the mourners tears.

Bless us all, both old and young;
Call forth praise from every tongue;
Let the whole assembly prove
All thy pow'r, and all thy love!

Hymn 10
John Newton
Casting the gospel net.

When Peter through the tedious night
Lk 5:4
Had often cast his net in vain;
Soon as his LORD appeared in sight
He gladly let it down again.

Once more the gospel net we cast,
Do thou, O LORD, the effort own;
We learn from disappointments past,
To rest our hope on thee alone.

Upheld by thy supporting hand,
We enter on another year;
And now we meet, at thy command,
To seek thy gracious presence here.

May this be a much favored hour,
To souls in Satan's bondage led!
O clothe thy word with sovereign pow'r
To break the rocks, and raise the dead!

Have mercy on our num'rous youth,
Who young in years, are old in sin;
And by thy Spirit, and thy truth,
Show them the state their souls are in.

Then, by a Savior's dying love
To every wounded heart revealed,
Temptations, fears, and guilt remove,
And be their Sun, and Strength, and Shield.

To mourners speak a cheering word,
On seeking souls vouchsafe to shine;
Let poor backsliders be restored,
And all thy saints in praises join.

O hear our prayer and give us hope,
That when thy voice shall call us home,
Thou still wilt raise a people up,
To love and praise thee in our room.

Hymn 11
William Cowper
Pleading for and with youth.

Sin has undone our wretched race,
But JESUS has restored
And brought the sinner face to face
With his forgiving LORD.

This we repeat from year to year,
And press upon our youth;
LORD, give them an attentive ear,
LORD, save them by thy truth.

Blessings upon the rising race!
Make this an happy hour,
According to thy richest grace,
And thine almighty pow'r.

We feel for your unhappy state,
(May you regard it too)
And would awhile ourselves forget,
To pour out prayer for you.

We see, though you perceive it not,
Th' approaching, aweful doom;
O tremble at the solemn thought,
And flee the wrath to come!

Dear Savior, let this new-born year
Spread an alarm abroad;
And cry, in every careless ear,
"Prepare to meet thy God!"

Hymn 12
William Cowper
Prayer for children.

Gracious Lord, our children see,
By thy mercy we are free;
But shall these, alas! remain
Subjects still of Satan's reign?
Israel's young ones, when of old
Pharaoh threatened to withhold;
Ex 10:9
Then thy messenger said, "No;
Let the children also go."

When the angel of the Lord
Drawing forth his dreadful sword,
Slew, with an avenging hand,
All the first-born of the land:
Ex 12:13
Then thy peoples' doors he passed,
Where the bloody sign was placed;
Hear us, now, upon our knees,
Plead the blood of CHRIST for these!

LORD we tremble, for we know
How the fierce malicious foe;
Wheeling round his watchful flight,
Keeps them ever in his sight:
Spread thy pinions, King of kings!
Hide them safe beneath thy wings;
Lest the rav'nous bird of prey
Stoop, and bear the brood away.

Hymn 13
John Newton
The Shunemite.
2Ki 4:31

The Shunemite, oppressed with grief,
When she had lost the son she loved,
Went to Elisha for relief,
Nor vain her application proved.

He sent his servant on before
To lay a staff upon his head;
This he could do, but do no more,
He left him, as he found him, dead.

But when the LORD'S almighty pow'r
Wrought with the prophet's prayer, and faith,
The mother saw a joyful hour,
She saw her child restored from death.

Thus, like the weeping Shunemite,
For many, dead in sin we grieve;
Now, LORD, display thine arm of might,
Cause them to hear thy voice and live.

Thy preachers bear the staff in vain,
Though at thine own command we go;
LORD, we have tried, and tried again,
We find them dead, and leave them so.

Come then thyself--to every heart
The glory of thy name make known;
The means are our appointed part,
The pow'r and grace are thine alone.

Hymn 14
John Newton
ELIJAH's prayer.
1Ki 18

Does it not grief, and wonder move,
To think of Israel's shameful fall?
Who needed miracles to prove
Whether the LORD was GOD, or Baal!

Methinks I see Elijah stand,
His features glow with love and zeal,
In faith and prayer he lifts his hand,
And makes to heav'n his great appeal,

"O God! if I thy servant am,
If 'tis thy message fills my heart;
Now glorify thy holy name,
And show this people who thou art!"

He spake, and lo! a sudden flame
Consumed the wood, the dust, the stone;
The people struck, at once proclaim
"The LORD is GOD, the LORD alone."

Like him we mourn an aweful day,
When more for Baal, than GOD appear;
Like him, believers, let us pray,
And may the GOD of Israel hear!

Lord, if thy servant speaks thy truth,
If he indeed is sent by thee;
Confirm the word to all our youth,
And let them thy salvation see.

Now may thy Spirit's holy fire
Pierce every heart that hears thy word;
Consume each hurtful vain desire,
And make them know thou art the Lord.

Hymn 15
John Newton
Preaching to the dry bones.
Ezek 37

Preachers may, from Ezekiel's case,
Draw hope in this declining day,
A proof like this, of sovereign grace
Should chase our unbelief away.

When sent to preach to mould'ring bones,
Who could have thought he would succeed?
But well he knew, the LORD from stones
Could raise up Abram's chosen seed.

Can these be made a num'rous host,
And such dry bones new life receive?
The prophet answered, "LORD thou knowst
They shall, if thou commandment give."

Like him, around I cast my eye,
And O! what heaps of bones appear!
Like him, by JESUS sent, I'll try,
For he can cause the dead to hear.

Hear, ye dry bones, the Savior's word!
He, who when dying, gasped, "Forgive,"
That gracious, sinner-loving LORD,
Says, "Look to me, dry bones, and live."

Thou heav'nly wind awake and blow,
In answer to the prayer of faith;
Now thine almighty influence show,
And fill dry bones with living breath.

O make them hear, and feel, and shake,
And, at thy call, obedient move;
The bonds of death and Satan break,
And bone to bone unite in love.

Hymn 16
John Newton
The rod of MOSES.

When Moses waved his mystic rod
What wonders followed while he spoke?
Firm as a wall the waters stood,
Ex 14:21
Or gushed in rivers from the rock!
Num 20:11

At his command the thunders rolled,
Lightning and hail his voice obeyed;
Ex 9:23
And Pharaoh trembled, to behold
His land in desolation laid.

But what could Moses' rod have done
Had he not been divinely sent?
The pow'r was from the LORD alone,
And Moses but the instrument.

O Lord, regard thy peoples prayers!
Assist a worm to preach aright
And since thy gospel-rod he bears,
Display thy wonders in our sight.

Proclaim the thunders of thy law,
Like lightning let thine arrows fly,
That careless sinners, struck with awe,
For refuge may to JESUS cry!

Make streams of godly sorrow flow
From rocky hearts, unused to feel;
And let the poor in spirit know
That thou art near, their griefs to heal.

But chiefly, we would now look up
To ask a blessing for our youth,
The rising generation's hope,
That they may know and love thy truth.

Olney Hymns
Arise, O Lord, afford a sign,
Now shall our prayers success obtain;
Since both the means and pow'r are thine,
How can the rod be raised in vain!

Hymn 17
John Newton
GOD speaking from mount Zion.

The God who once to Israel spoke
From Sinai's top, in fire and smoke,
In gentler strains of gospel grace
Invites us, now, to seek his face.

He wears no terrors on his brow,
He speaks, in love, from Zion, now;
It is the voice of JESUS' blood
Calling poor wand'rers home to GOD.

The holy Moses quaked and feared
When Sinai's thund'ring law he heard;
But reigning grace, with accents mild,
Speaks to the sinner, as a child.

Hark! how from Calvary it sounds;
From the Redeemer's bleeding wounds!
"Pardon and grace, I freely give,
Poor sinner, look to me, and live."

What other arguments can move
The heart, that slights a Savior's love!
Yet till Almighty pow'r constrain,
This matchless love is preached in vain.

O Savior let that pow'r be felt,
And cause each stony heart to melt!
Deeply impress upon our youth
The light, and force, of gospel truth.

With this new-year may they begin
To live to thee, and die to sin,
To enter by the narrow way
Which leads to everlasting day.

How will they else thy presence bear
When as a Judge thou shalt appear!
When slighted love to wrath shall turn,
And the whole earth like Sinai burn!

Hymn 18
John Newton
A prayer for power on the means of grace.

O Thou, at whose almighty word,
The glorious light from darkness sprung!
Thy quick'ning influence afford,
And clothe with pow'r the preacher's tongue.

Though 'tis thy truth he hopes to speak,
He cannot give the hearing ear;
'Tis thine, the stubborn heart to break,
And make the careless sinner fear.

As when of old, the water flowed
Forth from the rock at thy command;
Num 20:11
Moses in vain had waved the rod,
Without thy wonder-working hand.

As when the walls of Jericho
Josh 6:20
Down to the earth at once were cast;
It was thy pow'r that brought them low,
And not the trumpets' feeble blast.

Thus we would in the means be found,
And thus, on thee alone, depend;
To make the gospel's joyful sound
Effectual, to the promised end.

Now, while we hear thy word of grace,
Let self and pride before it fall;
And rocky hearts dissolve apace,
In streams of sorrow at thy call.

On all our youth assembled here
The unction of thy Spirit pour;
Nor let them lose another year,
Lest thou shouldst strive and call no more.

Hymn 19
John Newton
ELIJAH's mantle.
2Ki 51:11-14

Elisha, struck with grief and awe,
Cried, "Ah! where now is Israel's stay?"
When he his honored master saw
Borne by a fiery carr away.

But while be looked a last adieu,
His mantle, as it fell, he caught;
The Spirit rested on him too,
And equal miracles he wrought.

"Where is Elijah's GOD," he cried,
And with the mantle smote the flood;
His word controlled the swelling tide,
Th' obedient waters upright stood.

The wonder-working gospel, thus
From hand to hand, has been conveyed
We have the mantle still with us,
But where, O where, the Spirit's aid?

When Peter first this mantle waved,
Acts 2
How soon it melted hearts of steel!
Sinners, by thousands, then were saved,
But now how few its virtues feel?

Where is Elijah's GOD, the LORD,
Thine Israel's hope, and joy, and boast!
Reveal thine arm, confirm thy word,
Give us another Pentecost!

Assist thy messenger to speak,
And while he aims to lisp thy truth,
The bonds of sin and Satan break,
And pour thy blessing on our youth.

For them we now approach thy throne,
Teach them to know and love thy name,
Then shall thy thankful people own
Elijah's God is still the same.

HYMNS after Sermons to young people, on new-years evenings, suited to the subjects

Hymn 20
John Newton
DAVID's charge to SOLOMON.
1Chr 28:9

O David's Son, and David's Lord!
From age to age thou art the same;
Thy gracious presence now afford,
And teach our youth to know thy name!

Thy people, LORD, though oft distressed,
Upheld by thee, thus far are come;
And now we long to see thy rest,
And wait thy word to call us home.

Like David, when this life shall end,
We trust in thee sure peace to find;
Like him, to thee we now commend
The children we must leave behind.

Ere long, we hope to be, where care,
And sin, and sorrow, never come
But O! accept our humble prayer,
That these may praise thee in our room.

Show them how vile they are by sin,
And wash them in thy cleansing blood;
O, make them willing to be thine,
And be, to them, a cov'nant God.

Long may thy light and truth remain
To bless this place, when we are gone;
And numbers here be born again,
To dwell for ever near thy throne.

Hymn 21
John Newton
The Lord's call to his children.
2Cor 6:17,18

Let us adore the grace that seeks
To draw our hearts above!
Attend, 'tis God the Savior speaks,
And every word is love.

Though filled with awe, before his throne
Each angel veils his face;
He claims a people for his own
Amongst our sinful race.

Careless, awhile, they live in sin,
Enslaved to Satan's pow'r;
But they obey the call divine,
In his appointed hour.

Come forth, he says, no more pursue
The paths that lead to death;
Look up, a bleeding Savior view,
Look, and be saved by faith.

My sons and daughters you shall be
Through the atoning blood;
And you shall claim, and find, in me,
A Father, and a God."

Lord, speak these words to every heart,
By thine all-powerful voice;
That we may now from sin depart,
And make thy love our choice.

If now, we learn to seek thy face
By Christ, the living way;
We'll praise thee for this hour of grace,
Through an eternal day.

Hymn 22
John Newton
The prayer of JABEZ.
1Chr 4:9,10

Jesus, who bought us with his blood,
And makes our souls his care;
Was known of old as Israel's GOD,
And answered Jabez' prayer.

Jabez! a child of grief! the name
Befits poor sinners well;
For Jesus bore the cross and shame,
To save our souls from hell.

Teach us, O Lord, like him, to plead
For mercies from above;
O come, and bless our souls indeed,
With light, and joy, and love.

The gospel's promised land is wide,
We fain would enter in;
But we are pressed, on every side,
With unbelief and sin.

Arise; O LORD, enlarge our coast,
Let us possess the whole;
That Satan may no longer boast
He can thy work control.

Oh, may thine hand be with us still,
Our Guide and Guardian be;
To keep us safe from every ill,
Till death shall set us free.

Help us on thee to cast our care,
And on thy word to rest;
That Israel's God, who heareth prayer,
Will grant us our request.

Hymn 23
John Newton
Waiting at Wisdom's gates.
Prov 8:34,35

Ensnared, too long, my heart has been
In folly's hurtful ways;
O, may I now, at length, begin
To hear what Wisdom says!

'Tis JESUS, from the mercy-seat,
Invites me to his rest;
He calls poor sinners to his feet
To make them truly blest.

Approach my soul to Wisdom's gates
While it is called today;
No one who watches there and waits
Shall e'er be turned away.

He will not let me seek in vain,
For all, who trust his word,
Shall everlasting life obtain,
And favor from the LORD.

LORD, I have hated thee too long,
And dared thee to thy face;
I've done my soul exceeding wrong
In slighting all thy grace.

Now I would break my league with death,
And live to thee alone;
O let thy Spirit's seal of faith,
Secure me for thine own.

Let all the saints assembled here,
Yea, let all heav'n rejoice;
That I begin with this new-year,
To make the LORD my choice.

Hymn 24
John Newton
Asking the way to Zion.
Jer 1:5

Zion! the city of our God,
How glorious is the place!
The Savior there has his abode,
And sinners see his face.

Firm, against every adverse shock,
Its mighty bulwarks prove
'Tis built upon the living Rock,
And walled around with love.

There, all the fruits of glory grow,
And joys that never die;
And streams of grace, and knowledge flow,
The soul to satisfy.

Come, set your faces Zion-ward,
The sacred road enquire;
And let a union to the LORD
Be henceforth your desire!

The gospel shines to give you light,
No longer, then, delay;
The Spirit waits to guide you right,
And JESUS is the way.

O Lord, regard thy peoples prayer,
Thy promise now fulfill;
And young and old, by grace prepare,
To dwell on Zion's hill.

Hymn 25
John Newton
We were PHARAOH's bondmen.
Deut 6:20-23

Beneath the tyrant Satan's yoke
Our souls were long oppressed;
Till grace our galling fetters broke,
And gave the weary rest.

Jesus, in that important hour,
His mighty arm made known;
He ransomed us by price, and pow'r,
And claimed us for his own.

Now, freed from bondage, sin, and death,
We walk in Wisdom's ways;
And wish to spend our every breath,
In wonder, love, and praise.

Ere long, we hope with him to dwell
In yonder world above;
And now, we only live to tell
The riches of his love.

O might we, ere we hence remove,
Prevail upon our youth
To seek, that they may likewise prove,
His mercy and his truth.

Like Simeon, we shall gladly go,
Lk 2:29
When JESUS calls us home;
If they are left a seed below,
To serve him in our room.

Lord hear our prayer, indulge our hope,
On these thy Spirit pour;
That they may take our story up,
When we can speak no more.

Hymn 26
John Newton
Travailing in birth for souls.
Gal 4:19

What contradictions meet
In ministers' employ!
It is a bitter sweet,
A sorrow full of joy:
No other post affords a place
For equal honor, or disgrace!

Who can describe the pain
Which faithful preachers feel;
Constrained to speak, in vain,
To hearts as hard as steel?
Or who can tell the pleasures felt,
When stubborn hearts begin to melt?

The Savior's dying love,
The soul's amazing worth;
Their utmost efforts move,
And draw their bowels forth:
They pray and strive, their rest departs,
Till CHRIST be formed in sinners hearts.

If some small hope appear,
They still are not content;
But, with a jealous fear,
They watch for the event:
Too oft they find their hopes deceived,
Then, how their inmost souls are grieved!

But when their pains succeed,
And from the tender blade
The rip'ning ears proceed,
Their toils are overpaid:
No harvest-joy can equal theirs,
To find the fruit of all their cares.

On what has now been sown
Thy blessing, LORD, bestow;

John Newton

The pow'r is thine alone,
To make it spring and grow:
Do thou the gracious harvest raise,
And thou, alone, shalt have the praise.

Hymn 27
John Newton
We are ambassadors for CHRIST
2 Cor 5:20

Thy message, by the preacher, seal,
And let thy pow'r be known;
That every sinner here, may feel
The word is not his own.

Amongst the foremost of the throng
Who dare thee to thy face,
He in rebellion stood too long,
And fought against thy grace.

But grace prevailed, he mercy found,
And now by thee is sent,
To tell his fellow-rebels round,
And call them to repent.

In Jesus, God is reconciled,
The worst may be forgiv'n;
Come, and he'll own you as a child,
And make you heirs of heav'n.

O, may the word of gospel truth
Your chief desires engage
And JESUS be your guide in youth,
Your joy in hoary age.

Perhaps the year, that's now begun,
May prove to some their last;
The sands of life may soon be run,
The day of grace be past.

Think, if you slight this embassy,
And will not warning take;
When Jesus in the clouds you see,
What answer will you make?

Hymn 28
John Newton
PAUL's farewell charge.
Acts 20:26,27

When Paul was parted from his friends
It was a weeping day;
But Jesus made them all amends,
And wiped their tears away.

Ere long they met again, with joy,
(Secure no more to part)
Where praises every tongue employ,
And pleasure fills each heart.

Thus all the preachers of his grace
Their children soon shall meet;
Together see their Savior's face,
And worship at his feet.

But they who heard the word in vain,
Though oft, and plainly, warned;
Will tremble, when they meet again
The ministers they scorned

On your own heads your blood will fall
If any perish here
The preachers, who have told you all,
Shall stand approved, and clear.

Yet, LORD, to save themselves alone,
Is not their utmost view;
Oh bear their prayer, thy message own,
And save their hearers too.

Hymn 29
John Newton
How shall I put thee among the children?
Jer 3:19

Alas! by nature how depraved,
How prone to every ill!
Our lives, to Satan, how enslaved,
How obstinate our will!

And can such sinners be restored,
Such rebels reconciled?
Can grace itself the means afford
To make a foe a child?

Yes, grace has found the wondrous means
Which shall effectual prove;
To cleanse us from our countless sins,
And teach our hearts to love.

Jesus for sinners undertakes,
And died that we may live;
His blood a full atonement makes,
And cries aloud, "Forgive."

Yet one thing more must grace provide,
To bring us home to God;
Or we shall slight the LORD, who died,
And trample on his blood.

The holy Spirit must reveal
The Savior's work and worth;
Then the hard heart begins to feel
A new and heavenly birth.

Thus bought with blood, and born again,
Redeemed, and saved, by grace
Rebels, in God's own house obtain
A son's and daughter's place.

Hymn 30
John Newton
Winter[20]

See, how rude winter's icy hand
Has stripped the trees, and sealed the ground!
But spring shall soon his rage withstand,
And spread new beauties all around.

My soul, a sharper winter mourns,
Barren and fruitless I remain;
When will the gentle spring return,
And bid my graces grow again?

Jesus, my glorious Sun arise!
'Tis thine, the frozen heart to move
O hush these storms and clear my skies,
And let me feel thy vital love!

Dear Lord, regard my feeble cry,
I faint and droop till thou appear;
Wilt thou permit thy plant to die?
Must it be winter all the year?

Be still, my soul, and wait his hour,
With humble prayer, and patient faith;
Till he reveals his gracious pow'r,
Repose on what his promise faith.

He, by whose all-commanding word,
Gen 8:22
Seasons this changing course maintain;
In every change a pledge affords,
That none shall seek his face in vain.

Footnotes:
20. See also Book 3, Hymn 31

Hymn 31
John Newton
Waiting for Spring.

Though cloudy skies, and northern blasts,
Retard the gentle spring awhile;
The sun will conqu'ror prove at last,
And nature wear a vernal smile.

The promise, which from age to age,
Has brought the changing seasons round;
Again shall calm the winter's rage,
Perfume the air, and paint the ground.

The virtue of that first command,
I know still does, and will prevail;
That while the earth itself shall stand,
The spring and summer shall not fail.

Such changes are for us decreed;
Believers have their winters too;
But spring shall certainly succeed,
And all their former life renew.

Winter and spring have each their use,
And each, in turn, his people know;
One kills the weeds their hearts produce,
The other makes their graces grow.

Though like dead trees awhile they seem,
Yet having life within their root,
The welcome spring's reviving beam
Draws forth their blossoms, leaves, and fruit.

But if the tree indeed be dead,
It feels no change, though spring return,
Its leafless naked, barren head,
Proclaims it only fit to burn.

Dear LORD, afford our souls a spring,
Thou know'st our winter has been long;
Shine forth, and warm our hearts to sing,
And thy rich grace shall be our song.

Hymn 32
John Newton
Spring.

Bleak winter is subdued at length,
And forced to yield the day;
The sun has waited all his strength,
And driven him away.

And now long wished for spring is come,
How altered is the scene!
The trees and shrubs are dressed in bloom,
The earth arrayed in green.

Where'er we tread, beneath our feet
The clust'ring flowers spring;
The artless birds, in concert sweet,
Invite our hearts to sing.

But ah! in vain I strive to join,
Oppressed with sin and doubt;
I feet 'tis winter still, within,
Though all is spring without.

O! would my Savior from on high,
Break through these clouds and shine!
No creature then, more blest than I,
No song more loud than mine.

Till then--no softly warbling thrush,
Nor cowslip's sweet perfume;
Nor beauties of each painted bush,
Can dissipate my gloom.

To Adam, soon as he transgressed,
Thus Eden bloomed in vain;
Not paradise could give him rest,
Or soothe his heart-felt pain.

Yet here an emblem I perceive
Of what the LORD can do;
Dear Savior, help me to believe
That I may flourish too.

Olney Hymns
Thy word can soon my hopes revive,
Can overcome my foes;
And make my languid graces thrive,
And blossom like the rose.

Hymn 33
John Newton
Spring.

Pleasing spring again is here!
Trees and fields in bloom appear;
Hark! the birds, with artless lays,
Warble their Creator's praise!
Where, in winter, all was snow,
Now the flow'rs in clusters grow;
And the corn, in green array,[21]
Promises a harvest-day.

What a change has taken place!
Emblem of the spring of grace;
How the soul, in winter, mourns
Till the LORD, the Sun, returns;
Till the Spirit's gentle rain,
Bids the heart revive again;
Then the stone is turned to flesh,
And each grace springs forth afresh.

LORD, afford a spring to me!
Let me feel like what I see;
Ah! my winter has been long,
Chilled my hopes, and stopped my song!
Winter threatened to destroy
Faith, and love, and every joy;
If thy life was in the root,
Still I could not yield thee fruit.

Speak, and by thy gracious voice
Make my drooping soul rejoice;
O beloved Savior, haste,
Tell me all the storms are past:
On thy garden deign to smile,
Raise the plants, enrich the soil;
Soon thy presence will restore
Life, to what seemed dead before.

LORD, I long to be at home,
Where these changes never come!
Where the saints no winter fear,
Where 'tis spring throughout the year:
How unlike this state below!

Olney Hymns
There the flow'rs unwith'ring blow,
There no chilling blasts annoy,
All is love, and bloom, and joy.

Footnotes:
21. corn: i.e. wheat

Hymn 34
John Newton
Summer-forms.[22]

Though the morn may be serene,
Not a threat'ning cloud be seen;
Who can undertake to say
'Twill be pleasant all the day?
Tempests suddenly may rise,
Darkness overspread the skies;
Lightnings flash, and thunders roar,
Ere a short-lived day be o'er.

Often thus, the child of grace,
Enters on his christian race;
Guilt and fear are overborne,
'Tis with him a summer's morn:
While his new-felt joys abound,
All things seem to smile around;
And he hopes it will be fair,
All the day, and all the year.

Should we warn him of a change,
He would think the caution strange;
He no change or trouble fears,
Till the gath'ring storm appears;[23]
Till dark clouds his sun conceal,
Till temptation's pow'r he feel;
Then he trembles, and looks pale,
All his hopes and courage fail.

But the wonder-working Lord
Soothes the tempest by his word;
Stills the thunder, stops the rain,
And his sun breaks forth again:
Soon the cloud again returns,
Now he joys, and now he mourns;
Oft his sky is overcast,
Ere the day of life be past.

Tried believers too can say,
In the course of one short day,
Though the morning has been fair,
Proved a golden hour of prayer:
Sin, and Satan, long ere night,

Olney Hymns
Have their comforts put to flight;
Ah! what heart-felt peace and joy,
Unexpected storms destroy.

Dearest Savior, call us soon
To thine high eternal noon;
Never there shall tempest rise
To conceal thee from our eyes:
Satan shall no more deceive,
We no more thy Spirit grieve;
But through cloudless, endless days,
Sound, to golden harps, thy praise.

Footnotes:
22. See also Book 3, Hymn 68
23. See also Book 1, Hymn 44

Hymn 35
John Newton
Hay-time.

The grass, and flow'rs, which clothe the field,
And look so green and gay;
Touched by the scythe, defenseless yield,
And fall, and fade away.

Fit emblem of our mortal state!
Thus in the scripture glass,
The young, the strong, the wise, the great,
May see themselves but grass;
Isa 40:7

Ah! trust not to your fleeting breath,
Nor call your time your own;
Around you, see, the scythe of death
Is mowing thousands down.

And you, who hitherto are spared,
Must shortly yield your lives;
Your wisdom is to be prepared,
Before the stroke arrives.

The grass, when dead, revives no more,
You die, to live again;
But o! if death should prove the door
To everlasting pain.

Lord, help us to obey thy call,
That from our sins set free
When like the grass our bodies fall,
Our souls may spring to thee.

Hymn 36
John Newton
Harvest.

See! the corn again in ear!
How the fields and valleys smile!
Harvest now is drawing near
To repay the farmer's toil:
Gracious LORD, secure the crop,
Satisfy the poor with food;
In thy mercy is our hope,
We have sinned but thou art good.

While I view the plenteous grain
As it ripens on the stalk;
May I not instruction gain,
Helpful, to my daily walk?
All this plenty of the field
Was produced from foreign seeds;
For the earth itself would yield
Only crops of useless weeds.

Though, when newly sawn, it lay
Hid awhile beneath the ground,
(Some might think it thrown away)
Now a large increase is found:
Though concealed, it was not lost,
Though it died, it lives again;
Eastern storms, and nipping frosts
Have opposed its growth in vain.

Let the praise be all the Lord's,
As the benefit is ours!
He, in seasons, still affords
Kindly heat, and gentle flow'rs:
By his care the produce thrives
Waving o'er the furrowed lands;
And when harvest-time arrives,
Ready for the reaper stands.

Thus in barren hearts he sows
Precious seeds of heav'nly joy;
Hos 14:7 Mk 4:26-29
Sin, and hell, in vain oppose,
None can grace's crop destroy:

John Newton

Threatened oft, yet still it blooms,
After many changes past,
Death, the reaper, when he comes,
Finds it fully ripe at last.

CHRISTMAS

Hymn 37
John Newton
Praise for the incarnation.

Sweeter founds than music knows
Charm me, in EMMANUEL'S name;
All her hopes my spirit owes
To his birth, and cross, and shame.

When he came the angels sang
"Glory be to GOD on high,"
Lord, unloose my stamm'ring tongue,
Who should louder sing than I.

Did the Lord a man become
That he might the law fulfil,
Bleed and suffer in my room,
And canst thou, my tongue, be still.

No, I must my praises bring,
Though they worthless are, and weak;
For should I refuse to sing
Sure the very stones would speak.

O my Savior, Shield, and Sun,
Shepherd, Brother, Husband, Friend,
Every precious name in one;
I will love thee without end.

John Newton

Hymn 38
William Cowper
JEHOVAH-JESUS.

My song shall bless the LORD of all,
My praise shall climb to his abode;
Thee, Savior, by that name I call,
The great Supreme, the mighty GOD.

Without beginning, or decline,
Object of faith, and not of sense;
Eternal ages saw him shine,
He shines eternal ages hence.

As much, when in the manger laid,
Almighty ruler of the sky;
As when the six days' works he made,
Filled all the morning-stars with joy.

Of all the crowns JEHOVAH bears,
Salvation is his dearest claim;
That gracious sound well-pleased he hears,
And owns EMMANUEL for his name.

A cheerful confidence I feel,
My well-placed hopes with joy I see;
My bosom glows with heav'nly zeal
To worship him who died for me.

As man, he pities my complaint,
His pow'r and truth are all divine;
He will not fail, he cannot faint,
Salvation's sure, and must be mine.

Hymn 39
John Newton
Man honored above angels.

Now let us join with hearts and tongues,
And emulate the angels' songs;
Yea, sinners may address their King
In songs that angels cannot sing.

They praise the Lamb who once was slain,
But we can add a higher strain;
Rev 5
Not only say, "He suffered thus,"
But, that he suffered all for us.

When angels by transgression fell,
Justice consigned them all to hell;
But mercy formed a wondrous plan,
To save, and honor fallen man.

Jesus, who passed the angels by,
Heb 2:16
Assumed our flesh to bleed and die;
And still he makes it his abode,
As man, he fills the throne of God.

Our next of kin, our Brother now,
Is he to whom the angels bow;
They join with us to praise his name,
But we the nearest interest claim.

But ah! how faint our praises rise!
Sure, 'tis the wonder of the skies;
That we, who share his richest love,
So cold and unconcerned should prove.

O glorious hour it comes with speed
When we from sin and darkness freed,
Shall see the GOD who died for man,
And praise him more than angels can.[24]

Footnotes:
24. See also Book 3, Hymn 83

Hymn 40

John Newton
Saturday evening.

Safely through another week,
GOD has brought us on our way,
Let us now a blessing seek
On th' approaching sabbath-day:
Day, of all the week, the best;
Emblem of eternal rest!

Mercies, multiplied each hour,
Through the week our praise demand;
Guarded by almighty pow'r,
Fed and guided by his hand:
Though ungrateful we have been,
Only made returns of sin.

While we pray for pard'ning grace,
Through the dear Redeemer's name;
Show thy reconciled face,
Shine away our sin and shame:
From our worldly cares set free,
May we rest, this night, with thee.

When the morn shall bid us rise,
May we feel thy presence near;
May thy glory meet our eyes,
When we in thy house appear!
There afford us, LORD, a taste
Of our everlasting feast.

May thy gospel's joyful sound
Conquer sinners, comfort saints;
Make the fruits of grace abound,
Bring relief for all complaints:
Thus may all our Sabbaths prove
Till we join the church above!

THE CLOSE OF THE YEAR

Hymn 41
John Newton
EBENEZER
1Sam 7:12

The LORD, our salvation and light,
The guide and the strength of our days;
Has brought us together, tonight,
A new Ebenezer to raise:
The year, we have now passed through,
His goodness with blessings has crowned;
Each morning his mercies were new,
Then let our thanksgivings abound.

Encompassed with dangers and snares,
Temptations, and fears, and complaints;
His ear he inclined to our prayers,
His hand opened wide to our wants:
We never besought him in vain,
When burdened with sorrow or sin,
He helped us again and again,
Or where, before now, had we been?

His gospel, throughout the long year,
From Sabbath to Sabbath he gave;
How oft has he met with us here,
And shown himself mighty to save?
His candlestick has been removed
From churches once privileged thus;
But, though we unworthy have proved,
It still is continued to us.

For so many mercies received,
Alas! what returns have we made?
His Spirit we often have grieved,
And evil, for good, have repaid:
How well it becomes us to cry,
"O, who is a GOD like to thee?
Who passest iniquities by,
And plungest them deep in the sea!"

John Newton

To JESUS, who sits on the throne,
Our best hallelujahs we bring;
To thee it is owing alone,
That we are permitted to sing:
Assist us, we pray, to lament
The sins of the year that is past;
And grant that the next may be spent
Far more to thy praise than the last.

Hymn 42
John Newton
EBENEZER
1Sam 7:12

Let hearts and tongues unite
And loud thanksgivings raise;
'Tis duty, mingled with delight,
The Savior's name to praise.

To him we owe our breath,
He took us from the womb,
Which else had shut us up in death,
And proved an early tomb.

When on the breast we hung
Our help was in the Lord;
'Twas he first taught our infant tongue
To form the lisping word.

When in our blood we lay
He would not let us die,
Because his love had fixed a day
To bring salvation nigh.

In childhood and in youth
His eye was on us still;
Though strangers to his love and truth,
And prone to cross his will.

And since his name we knew,
How gracious has he been!
What dangers has he led us through,
What mercies have we seen!

Now through another year
Supported by his care;
We raise our Ebenezer here,
"The LORD has helped thus far."

Our lot in future years
Unable to foresee
He, kindly to prevent our fears,
Says, "Leave it all to me."

John Newton

Yea, LORD, we wish to cast
Our cares upon thy breast!
Help us to praise thee for the past,
And trust thee for the rest.

II. ORDINANCES

Hymn 43
John Newton
On opening a place for social prayer.

O LORD, our languid souls inspire,
For here, we trust, thou art!
Send down a coal of heav'nly fire,
To warm each waiting heart.

Dear Shepherd of thy people, hear,
Thy presence now display;
As thou hast giv'n a place for prayer,
So give us hearts to pray.

Show us some token of thy love,
Our fainting hope to raise;
And pour thy blessings from above,
That we may render praise.

Within there walls let holy peace,
And love, and concord dwell;
Here give the troubled conscience ease,
The wounded spirit heal.

The feeling heart, the melting eye,
The humble mind bestow;
And shine upon us from on high,
To make our graces grow!

May we in faith receive thy word,
In faith present our prayers;
And, in the presence of our LORD,
Unbosom all our cares.

And may the gospel's joyful sound
Enforced by mighty grace,
Awaken many sinners round,
To come and fill the place.

Hymn 44
William Cowper
On opening a place for social prayer.

Jesus, where'er thy people meet,
There they behold thy mercy-seat;
Where'er they seek thee thou art found,
And every place is hallowed ground.

For thou, within no walls confined,
Inhabitest the humble mind;
Such ever bring thee, where they come,
And going, take thee to their home.

Dear Shepherd of thy chosen few
Thy former mercies here renew;
Here, to our waiting hearts, proclaim
The sweetness of thy saving name.

Here may we prove the pow'r of prayer,
To strengthen faith, and sweeten care;
To teach our faint desires to rise
And bring all heav'n before our eyes.

Behold at thy commanding word,
We stretch the curtain and the cord;
Isa 54:2
Come thou, and fill this wider space,
And bless us with a large increase.

LORD, we are few, but thou art near;
Nor short thine arm, nor deaf thine ear;
Oh rend the heav'ns, come quickly down,
And make a thousand hearts thine own!

Hymn 45
John Newton
The Lord's day.

How welcome to the saints, when pressed
With six days noise, and care, and toil,
Is the returning day of rest,
Which hides them from the world awhile?

Now, from the throng withdrawn away,
They seem to breathe a different air;
Composed and softened by the day,
All things another aspect wear.

How happy if their lot is cast,
Where statedly the gospel sounds
The word is honey to their taste,
Renews their strength, and heals their wounds!

Though pinched with poverty at home,
With sharp afflictions daily fed;
It makes amends, if they can come
To GOD'S own house for heav'nly bread!

With joy they hasten to the place,
Where they their Savior oft have met;
And while they feast upon his grace,
Their burdens and their griefs forget.

This favored lot, my friends, is curs,
May we the privilege improve;
And find these consecrated hours,
Sweet earnests of the joys above!

We thank thee for thy day, O Lord,
Here we thy promised presence seek;
Open thine hand, with blessings stored,
And give us Manna for the week.

John Newton

Hymn 46
John Newton
Gospel privileges.

O happy they who know the Lord,
With whom he deigns to dwell!
He feeds and cheers them by his word,
His arm supports them well.

To them, in each distressing hour,
His throne of grace is near;
And when they plead his love and pow'r,
He stands engaged to hear.

He helped his saints in ancient days
Who trusted in his name;
And we can witness, to his praise,
His love is still the same.

Wand'ring in sin, our souls he found,
And bid us seek his face;
Gave us to hear the gospel sound,
And taste the gospel grace.

Oft in his house his glory shines
Before our wond'ring eyes;
We wish not, then, for golden mines,
Or ought beneath the skies.

His presence sweetens all our cares,
And makes our burdens light;
A word from him dispels our fears,
And gilds the gloom of night.

Lord, we expect to suffer here,
Nor would we dare repine;
But give us, still, to find thee near;
And own us, still, for thine.

Let us enjoy, and highly prize
These tokens of thy love;
Till thou shalt bid our spirits rise,
To worship thee above.

Hymn 47
John Newton
Gospel privileges.

Happy are they, to whom the LORD
His gracious name makes known!
And by his Spirit, and his word,
Adopts them for his own!

He calls them to his mercy-seat,
And hears their humble prayer;
And when within his house they meet,
They find his presence near.

The force of their united cries
No pow'r can long withstand
For JESUS helps them from the skies,
By his almighty hand.

Then mountains sink at once to plains,
And light from darkness springs;
Each seeming loss improves their gains,
Each trouble comfort brings.

Though men despise them, or revile,
They count the trial small;
Whoever frowns, if JESUS smile,
It makes amends for all.

Though meanly clad, and coarsely fed,
And, like their Savior, poor;
They would not change their gospel bread
For all the worldling's store.

When cheered with faith's sublimer joys,
They mount on eagle's wings;
They can disdain, as children's toys,
The pride and pomp of kings.

Dear Lord, assist our souls to pay
The debt of praise we owe;
That we enjoy a gospel day,
And heav'n begun below.

Hymn 48

John Newton
Prayer for the continuance of the gospel[25]

Once, while we aimed at Zion's songs,
A sudden mourning checked our tongues!
Then we were called to sow in tears,
The seeds of joy for future years.

Oft as that memorable hour
The changing year brings round again;
We meet to praise the love and pow'r
Which heard our cries, and eased our pain.

Come, ye who trembled for the ark,
Unite in praise for answered prayer!
Did not the LORD our sorrows mark?
Did not our sighing reach his ear?

Then smaller griefs were laid aside,
And all our cares summed up in one;
"Let us but have thy word, we cried,
In other things, thy will be done."

Since he has granted our request,
And we still hear the gospel voice;
Although by many trials pressed,
In this we can, and will rejoice.

Though to our lot temptations fall,
Though pain and want, and cares annoy;
The precious gospel sweetens all,
And yields us med'cine, food, and joy.

Footnotes:

25. Wherever a separation is threatened between a minister and people who dearly love each other, this hymn may be as seasonable as it was once in Olney.

Hymn 49
John Newton
A famine of the word.

Gladness was spread through Israel's host
When first they Manna viewed;
They labored who should gather most,
And thought it pleasant food.

But when they had it long enjoyed
From day to day, the same;
Their hearts were by the plenty cloyed,
Although from heav'n it came.

Thus gospel bread at first is prized,
And makes a people glad;
But afterwards too much despised,
When easy to be had.

But should the Lord, displeased, withhold
The bread his mercy sends;
To have our houses filled with gold
Would make but poor amends.

How tedious would the week appear,
How dull the Sabbath prove?
Could we no longer meet to bear
The precious truths we love!

How would believing parents bear
To leave their heedless youth,
Exposed to every fatal snare,
Without the light of truth?

The gospel, and a praying few
Our bulwark long have proved;
But Olney sure the day will rue
When these shall be removed.

Then sin, in this once favored town,
Will triumph unrestrained;
And wrath and vengeance hasten down,
No more by prayer detained.

John Newton

Preserve us from this judgment, Lord
For JESUS' sake we plead;
A famine of the gospel word
Would be a stroke indeed!

Hymn 50

John Newton
Prayer for ministers.

Chief Shepherd of thy chosen sheep,
From death and sin set free;
May every under-shepherd keep
His eye, intent on thee!

With plenteous grace their hearts prepare,
To execute thy will
Compassion, patience, love and care,
And faithfulness and skill.

Inflame their minds with holy zeal
Their flocks to feed and teach;
And let them live, and let them feel
The sacred truths they preach.

Oh, never let the sheep complain
That toys, which fools amuse;
Ambition, pleasure, praise or gain,
Debase the shepherd's views.

He, that for these, forbears to feed
The souls whom JESUS loves;
Whate'er he may profess, or plead,
An idol-shepherd proves.
Zech 11:17

The sword of God shall break his arm,
A blast shall blind his eye
His word shall have no pow'r to warm,
His gifts shall all grow dry.

O LORD, avert this heavy woe,
Let all thy shepherds say!
And grace, and strength, on each bestow,
To labor while 'tis day.

Hymn 51
John Newton
Prayer for a revival

Savior, visit thy plantation,
Grant us, LORD, a gracious rain!
All will come to desolation,
Unless thou return again:
Keep no longer at a distance,
Shine upon us from on high;
Lest, for want of thine assistance;
Every plant would droop and die.

Surely, once thy garden flourished,
Every part looked gay and green;
Then thy word our spirits nourished,
Happy seasons we have seen!
But a drought has since succeeded,
And a sad decline we see;
LORD, thy help is greatly needed,
Help can only come from thee.

Where are those we counted leaders,
Filled with zeal, and love, and truth?
Old professors, tall as cedars,
Bright examples to our youth!
Some, in whom we once delighted,
We shall meet no more below;
Some, alas! we fear are blighted,
Scarce a single leaf they show.

Younger plants-the sight how pleasant,
Covered thick with blossoms stood;
But they cause us grief at present,
Frosts have nipped them in the bud!
Dearest Savior, hasten hither,
Thou canst make them bloom again;
O, permit them not to wither,
Let not all our hopes be vain!

Let our mutual love be fervent,
Make us prevalent in prayers;
Let each one esteemed thy servant,

Olney Hymns
Shun the world's bewitching snares:
Break the tempter's fatal power,
Turn the stony heart to flesh;
And begin, from this good hour,
To revive thy work afresh.

Hymn 52
John Newton
Hoping for a revival

My harp untuned, and laid aside,
(To cheerful hours the harp belongs)
My cruel foes, insulting cried,
"Come, sing us one of Zion's songs."

Alas! when sinners, blindly bold,
At Zion scoff, and Zion's King;
When zeal declines, and love grows cold,
Is this a day for me to sing?

Time was, whene'er the saints I met,
With joy and praise my bosom glowed;
But now, like Eli, sad I sit,
And tremble for the ark of God.

While thus to grief my soul gave way,
To see the work of GOD decline;
Methought I heard my Savior say,
"Dismiss thy fears, the ark is mine.

Though for a time I hide my face,
Rely upon my love and pow'r;
Still wrestle at a throne of grace,
And wait for a reviving hour.

Take down thy long neglected harp,
I've seen thy tears, and heard thy prayer;
The winter season has been sharp,
But spring shall all its wastes repair."

LORD, I obey, my hopes revive,
Come join with me, ye saints, and sing;
Our foes in vain against us strive;
For God will help and healing bring.

SACRAMENTAL HYMNS

Hymn 53
William Cowper
Welcome to the table.

This is the feast of heav'nly wine,
And God invites to sup;
The juices of the living vine
Were pressed, to fill the cup.

Oh, bless the Savior, ye that eat,
With royal dainties fed;
Not heav'n affords a costlier treat,
For JESUS is the bread!

The vile, the lost, he calls to them,
Ye trembling souls appear!
The righteous, in their own esteem,
Have no acceptance here.

Approach ye poor, nor dare refuse
The banquet spread for you;
Dear Savior, this is welcome news,
Then I may venture too.

If guilt and sin afford a plea,
And may obtain a place;
Surely the LORD will welcome me;
And I shall see his face.

Hymn 54
John Newton
CHRIST crucified.

When on the cross, my Lord I see
Bleeding to death, for wretched me;
Satan and sin no more can move,
For I am all transformed to love.

His thorns, and nails, pierce through my heart,
In every groan I bear a part;
I view his wounds with streaming eyes,
But see! he bows his head and dies!

Come, sinners, view the Lamb of God,
Wounded and dead, and bathed in blood!
Behold his side, and venture near,
The well of endless life is here.

Here I forget my cares and pains;
I drink, yet still my thirst remains;
Only the fountain-head above,
Can satisfy the thirst of love.

O, that I thus could always feel!
Lord, more and more thy love reveal!
Then my glad tongue shall loud proclaim
The grace and glory of thy name.

Thy name dispels my guilt and fear,
Revives my heart, and charms my ear;
Affords a balm for every wound,
And Satan trembles at the sound.

Hymn 55
William Cowper
Jesus hasting to suffer.

The Savior! what a noble flame
Was kindled in his breast,
When hasting to Jerusalem
He marched before the rest!

Good-will to men, and zeal for God,
His every thought engross;
He longs to be baptized with blood,
Lk 11:50
He pants to reach the cross.

With all his suff'rings full in view,
And woes, to us, unknown,
Forth to the task his spirit flew,
'Twas love that urged him on.

LORD, we return thee what we can!
Our hearts shall sound abroad
Salvation, to the dying Man,
And to the rising God!

And while thy bleeding glories here
Engage our wond'ring eyes;
We learn our lighter cross to bear,
And hasten to the skies.

Hymn 56
John Newton
It is good to be here.

Let me dwell on Golgotha,
Weep and love my life away!
While I see him on the tree
Weep and bleed, and die for me!

That dear blood, for sinners spilt,
Shows my sin in all its guilt:
Ah, my soul, he bore thy load,
Thou hast slain the Lamb of GOD.

Hark! his dying words; "Forgive,
Father, let the sinner live;
Sinner, wipe thy tears away,
I thy ransom freely pay."

While I hear this grace revealed,
And obtain a pardon sealed;
All my lost affections move,
Wakened by the force of love.

Farewell world, thy gold is dross,
Now I see the bleeding cross;
JESUS died to set me free
From the law, and sin, and thee!

He has dearly bought my soul
LORD, accept, and claim the whole!
To thy will I all resign,
Now, no more my own, but thine.

Hymn 57
John Newton
Looking at the cross.

In evil long I took delight,
Unawed by shame or fear;
Till a new object struck my sight,
And stopped my wild career.

I saw one hanging on a tree,
In agonies and blood;
Who fixed his languid eyes on me,
As near his cross I stood.

Sure, never till my latest breath,
Can I forget that look;
It seemed to charge me with his death,
Though not a word he spoke.

My conscience felt, and owned the guilt,
And plunged me in despair;
I saw my sins his blood had spilt,
And helped to nail him there.

Alas! I knew not what I did,
But now my tears are vain;
Where shall my trembling soul be hid?
For I the LORD have slain.

A second look he gave, which said,
"I freely all forgive;
This blood is for thy ransom paid,
I die, that thou may'st live."

Thus, while his death my sin displays,
In all its blackest hue;
(Such is the mystery of grace)
It seals my pardon too.

With pleasing grief and mournful joy,
My spirit now is filled;
That I should such a life destroy,
Yet live by him I killed.

Hymn 58
John Newton
Supplies in the wilderness.

When Israel by divine command
The pathless desert trod;
They found, though 'twas a barren land,
A sure resource in God.

A cloudy pillar marked their road,
And screened them from the heat;
From the hard rocks their water flowed,
And Manna was their meat.

Like them we have a rest in view,
Secure from adverse pow'rs;
Like them we pass a desert too,
But Israel's God is ours.

Yes, in this barren wilderness
He is to us the same;
By his appointed means of grace,
As once he was to them.

His word a light before us spreads
By which our path we see;
His love a banner o'er our head,
From harm preserves us free.

Lord, 'tis enough; I ask no more,
These blessings are divine;
I envy not the worldling's store,
If CHRIST and heav'n are mine.

Hymn 59
John Newton
Communion with the saints in glory.

Refreshed by the bread and wine,
The pledges of our Savior's love;
Now let our hearts and voices join
In songs of praise with those above.

Do they sing, "Worthy is the Lamb?"
Although we cannot reach their strains,
Yet we, through grace, can sing the same,
For us he died, for us he reigns.

If they behold him face to face,
While we a glimpse can only see;
Yet equal debtors to his grace,
As safe and as beloved are we.

They had, like us a suff'ring time,
Our cares and fears, and griefs they knew;
But they have conquered all through him,
And we, ere long, shall conquer too.

Though all the songs of saints in light,
Are far beneath his matchless worth;
His grace is such, he will not slight
The poor attempts of worms on earth.

ON PRAYER

Hymn 60
William Cowper
Exhortation to prayer.

What various hindrances we meet
In coming to a mercy-seat?
Yet who that knows the worth of prayer,
But wishes to be often there.

Prayer makes the darkened cloud withdraw,
Prayer climbs the ladder Jacob saw;
Gives exercise to faith and love,
Brings every blessing from above.

Restraining prayer, we cease to fight;
Prayer makes the christian's armor bright;
And Satan trembles, when he sees
The weakest saint upon his knees.

While Moses stood with arms spread wide,
Success was found on Israel's side;
Ex 17:11
But when through weariness they failed,
That moment Amalek prevailed.

Have you no words? ah, think again,
Words flow apace when you complain;
And fill your fellow-creature's ear
With the sad tale of all your care.

Were half the breath thus vainly spent,
To heav'n in supplication sent;
Your cheerful song would oft'ner be,
Hear what the LORD has done for me

Hymn 61
John Newton
Power of prayer.

In themselves, as weak as worms,
How can poor believers stand;
When temptations, foes, and storms,
Press them close on every hand?

Weak, indeed, they feel they are,
But they know the throne of grace;
And the God, who answers prayer,
Helps them when they seek his face.

Though the Lord awhile delay,
Succor they at length obtain;
He who taught their hearts to pray,
Will not let them cry in vain.

Wrestling prayer can wonders do,
Bring relief in deepest straits;
Prayer can force a passage through
Iron bars and brazen gates.

Hezekiah on his knees
Proud Assyria's host subdued;
And when smitten with disease,
Had his life by prayer renewed.

Peter, though confined and chained,
Prayer prevailed and brought him out;
When Elijah prayed, it rained,
After three long years of drought.

We can likewise witness bear,
That the LORD is still the same,
Though we feared he would not hear,
Suddenly deliverance came.

For the wonders he has wrought,
Let us now our praises give;
And, by sweet experience taught,
Call upon him while we live.

John Newton

ON THE SCRIPTURE

Hymn 62
William Cowper
The light and glory of the word.

The Spirit breathes upon the word,
And brings the truth to sight;
Precepts and promises afford
A sanctifying light.

A glory gilds the sacred page,
Majestic like the sun
It gives a light to every age,
It gives, but borrows none.

The hand that gave it, still supplies
The gracious light and heat;
His truths upon the nations rise,
They rise, but never set.

Let everlasting thanks be thine
For such a bright display,
As makes a world of darkness shine
With beams of heav'nly day.

My soul rejoices to pursue
The steps of him I love;
Till glory breaks upon my view
In brighter worlds above.

Hymn 63
John Newton
The word more precious than gold.

Precious Bible! what a treasure
Does the word of God afford?
All I want for life or pleasure,
FOOD and MED'CINE, SHIELD and SWORD:
Let the world account me poor,
Having this I need no more.

FOOD to which the world's a stranger,
Here my hungry soul enjoys
Of excess there is no danger,
Though it fills, it never cloys:
On a dying CHRIST I feed,
He is meat and drink indeed.

When my faith is faint and sickly,
Or when Satan wounds my mind,
Cordials, to revive me quickly,
Healing MED'CINES here I find:
To the promises I flee,
Each affords a remedy.

In the hour of dark temptation
Satan cannot make me yield;
For the word of consolation
Is to me a mighty SHIELD
While the scripture-truths are sure,
From his malice I'm secure.

Vain his threats to overcome me,
When I take the Spirits' SWORD;
Then with ease I drive him from me.
Satan trembles at the word:
'Tis a sword for conquest made,
Keen the edge, and strong the blade.

Shall I envy then the miser
Doting on his golden store?
Sure I am, or should be, wiser,
I am Rich, 'tis he is Poor:
JESUS gives me in his word,
FOOD and MED'CINE, SHIELD and SWORD.

III. PROVIDENCES

Hymn 64
John Newton
On the commencement of hostilities in America.

The gath'ring clouds, with aspect dark,
A rising storm presage;
O! to be hid within the ark,
And sheltered from its rage!

See the commissioned angel frown!
Rev 16:1
That vial in his hand,
Filled with fierce wrath, is pouring down
Upon our guilty land!

Ye saints, unite in wrestling prayer;
If yet there may be hope;
Who knows but Mercy yet may spare,
And bid the angel stop!
1Sam 24:16

Already is the plague begun,
Num 16:46
And fired with hostile rage;
Brethren, by blood and interest one,
With brethren now engage.

Peace spreads her wings, prepared for flight,
And war, with flaming sword,
And hasty strides draws nigh, to fight
The battles of the LORD.

The first alarm, alas, how few,
While distant, seem to hear!
But they will hear, and tremble too,
When God shall send it near.

So thunder, o'er the distant hills,
Gives but a murm'ring sound,
But as the tempest spreads, it fills,
And makes the welkin sound.[26]

Olney Hymns
May we, at least, with one consent,
Fall low before the throne
With tears the nation's sins lament,
The churches, and our own.

The humble souls who mourn and pray,
The LORD approves and knows;
His mark secures them in the day
When vengeance strikes his foes.

Footnotes:
26. welkin: firmament, or atmosphere.

FAST-DAY HYMNS

Hymn 65
John Newton
Confession and Prayer. December 13, 1776.

O, may the pow'r which melts the rock
Be felt by all assembled here!
Or else our service will but mock
The GOD whom we profess to fear!

Lord, while thy judgments shake the land,
Thy peoples' eyes are fixed on thee!
We own thy just, uplifted hand,
Which thousands cannot, will not see.

How long hast thou bestowed thy care
On this indulged ungrateful spot?
While other nations, far and near,
Have envied and admired our lot.

Here peace and liberty have dwelt,
The glorious gospel brightly shone;
And oft our enemies have felt
That GOD has made our cause his own.

But ah! both heav'n and earth have heard
Our vile requital of his love!
We, whom like children he has reared,
Rebels against his goodness prove.
Isa 1:2

His grace despised, his pow'r defied,
And legions of the blackest crimes,
Profaneness, riot, run, and pride,
Are signs that mark the present times.

The Lord, displeased, has raised his rod;
Ah where are now the faithful few
Who tremble for the ark of God,
And know what Israel ought to do?
1Chr 12:32

Olney Hymns
Lord, hear thy people everywhere,
Who meet to mourn, confess and pray;
The nation and thy churches spare,
And let thy wrath be turned away.

Hymn 66
John Newton
MOSES and AMALEK
February 27, 1778.
Ex 17:9

While Joshua led the armed bands.
Of Israel forth to war;
Moses apart with lifted hands
Engaged in humble prayer.

The armed bands had quickly failed,
And perished in the fight;
If Moses' prayer had not prevailed
To put the foes to flight.

When Moses' hands through weakness dropped,
The warriors fainted too;
Israel's success at once was stopped,
And Am'lek bolder grew.

A people, always prone to boast,
Were taught by this suspense,
That not a num'rous armed host,
But God was their defence.

We now of fleets and armies vaunt,
And ships and men prepare;
But men like Moses most we want,
To save the state by prayer.

Yet, Lord, we hope thou hast prepared
A hidden few today;
(The nation's secret strength and guard)
To weep, and mourn, and pray.

O hear their prayers and grant us aid,
Bid war and discord cease;
Heal the sad breach which sin has made,
And bless us all with peace.

Hymn 67
John Newton
The hiding place. February 10, 1779.

See the gloomy gath'ring cloud
Hanging o'er a sinful land!
Sure the LORD proclaims aloud,
Times of trouble are at hand:
Happy they, who love his name!
They shall always find him near;
Though the earth were wrapped in flame,
They have no just cause for fear.

Hark! his voice in accents mild,
(O, how comforting and sweet!)
Speaks to every humble child,
Pointing out a sure retreat!
Come, and in my chambers hide,
Isa 26:20
To my saints of old well known;
There you safely may abide,
Till the storm be overblown.

You have only to repose
On my wisdom, love, and care;
Where my wrath consumes my foes,
Mercy shall my children spare:
While they perish in the flood,
You that bear my holy mark,
Ezek 9:4
Sprinkled with atoning blood,
Shall be safe within the ark.

Sinners, see the ark prepared!
Haste to enter while there's room;
Though the Lord his arm has bared,
Mercy still retards your doom:
Seek him while there yet is hope,
Ere the day of grace be past;
Lest in wrath he give you up,
And this call should prove your last.

Hymn 68
John Newton
On the earthquake. September 8, 1775.

Although on massy pillars built,
The earth has lately shook;
It trembled under Britain's guilt,
Before its Maker's look.

Swift as the shock amazement spreads,
And sinners tremble too;
What flight can screen their guilty heads,
If earth itself pursue.

But mercy spared us while it warned,
The shock is felt no more;
And mercy, now, alas! is scorned
By sinners, as before.

But if these warnings prove in vain,
Say, sinner, canst thou tell,
How soon the earth may quake again,
And open wide to hell.

Repent before the Judge draws nigh;
Or else when he comes down,
Thou wilt in vain for earthquakes cry,
To hide thee from his frown.
Rev 6:16

But happy they who love the LORD
And his salvation know;
The hope that's founded on his word,
No change can overthrow.

Should the deep-rooted hills be hurled,
And plunged beneath the seas;
And strong convulsions shake the world,
Your hearts may rest in peace.

Jesus, your Shepherd, LORD, and Chief,
Shall shelter you from ill;
And not a worm or shaking leaf
Can move, but at his will.

Hymn 69
John Newton
On the fire at Olney. September 22, 1777.

Wearied by day with toils and cares,
How welcome is the peaceful night!
Sweet sleep our wasted strength repairs,
And fits us for returning light.

Yet when our eyes in sleep are closed,
Our rest may break ere well begun;
To dangers every hour exposed
We neither can foresee nor shun.

'Tis of the Lord that we can sleep
A single night without alarms;
His eye alone our lives can keep
Secure, amidst a thousand harms.

For months and years of safety past,
Ungrateful, we, alas! have been;
Though patient long, he spoke at last,
And bid the fire rebuke our sin.

The shout of fire! a dreadful cry,
Impressed each heart with deep dismay;
While the fierce blaze and red'ning sky,
Made midnight wear the face of day.

The throng and terror who can speak!
The various sounds that filled the air!
The infant's wail, the mother's shriek,
The voice of blasphemy and prayer!

But prayer prevailed, and saved the town;
The few, who loved the Savior's name,
Were heard, and mercy hasted down
To change the wind, and stop the flame.

O, may that night be ne'er forgot!
LORD, still increase thy praying few!
Were OLNEY left without a Lot,
Ruin, like Sodom's, would ensue.

Hymn 70
John Newton
A welcome to christian friends.

Kindred in CHRIST, for his dear sake,
A hearty welcome here receive;
May we together now partake
The joys which only he can give!

To you and us by grace 'tis giv'n,
To know the Savior's precious name;
And shortly we shall meet in heav'n,
Our hope, our way, our end, the same.

May he, by whose kind care we meet,
Send his good Spirit from above,
Make our communications sweet,
And cause our hearts to burn with love!

Forgotten be each worldly theme,
When christians see each other thus;
We only wish to speak of him,
Who lived, and died, and reigns for us.

We'll talk of all he did and said,
And suffered for us here below;
The path he marked for us to tread,
And what he's doing for us now.

Thus, as the moments pass away,
We'll love, and wonder, and adore;
And hasten on the glorious day,
When we shall meet to part no more.

Hymn 71
John Newton
At parting.

As the sun's enliv'ning eye
Shines on every place the same;
So the LORD is always nigh
To the souls that love his name.

When they move at duty's call,
He is with them by the way;
He is ever with them all,
Those who go, and those who stay.

From his holy mercy-seat
Nothing can their souls confine;
Still in spirit they may meet,
And in sweet communion join.

For a season called to part,
Let us then ourselves commend
To the gracious eye and heart,
Of our ever-present Friend.

Jesus, hear our humble prayer!
Tender Shepherd of thy sheep!
Let thy mercy and thy care
All our souls in safety keep.

In thy strength may we be strong,
Sweeten every cross and pain;
Give us, if we live, ere long
Here to meet in peace again.

Then, if thou thy help afford,
Ebenezers shall be reared;
And our souls shall praise the Lord
Who our poor petitions heard.

FUNERAL HYMNS

Hymn 72
John Newton
On the death of a believer.

In vain my fancy strives to paint
The moment after death
The glories that surround the saint,
When yielding up its breath.

One gentle sigh their fetters breaks,
We scarce can say, "They're gone!"
Before the willing spirit takes
Her mansion near the throne.

Faith strives, but all its efforts fail,
To trace her in her flight;
No eye can pierce within the veil
Which hides that world of light.

Thus much (and this is all) we know,
They are completely blest
Have done with sin, and care, and woe,
And with their Savior rest.

On harps of gold they praise his name,
His face they always view;
Then let us follow'rs be of them,
That we may praise him too.

Their faith and patience, love and zeal,
Should make their memory dear;
And, Lord, do thou the prayers fulfil,
They offered for us here

While they have gained, we losers are,
We miss them day by day;
But thou canst every breach repair,
And wipe our tears away.

Olney Hymns
We pray, as in Elisha's case,
When great Elijah went,
May double portions of thy grace,
To us who stay, be sent.

Hymn 73
William Cowper
On the death of a minister.

His master taken from his head,
Elisha saw him go;
And, in desponding accents said,
"Ah, what must Israel do!"

But he forgot the LORD, who lifts
The beggar to the throne;
Nor knew, that all Elijah's gifts
Would soon be made his own.

What! when a Paul has run his course,
Or when Apollos dies;
Is Israel left without resource?
And have we no supplies?

Yes, while the dear Redeemer lives,
We have a boundless store;
And shall be fed with what he gives,
Who lives for evermore.

Hymn 74
John Newton
The tolling bell

Oft as the bell, with solemn toll,
Speaks the departure of a soul;
Let each one ask himself; "Am I
Prepared, should I be called to die?"

Only this frail and fleeting breath
Preserves me from the jaws of death;
Soon as it fails, at once I'm gone,
And plunged into a world unknown.

Then, leaving all I loved below,
To GOD'S tribunal I must go;
Must hear the Judge pronounce my fate,
And fix my everlasting state.

But could I bear to hear him say,
"Depart, accursed, far away!
With Satan, in the lowest hell,
Thou art for ever doomed to dwell."

LORD JESUS! help me now to flee,
And seek my hope alone in thee.
Apply thy blood, thy Spirit give,
Subdue my sin, and in me live.

Then, when the solemn bell I hear,
If saved from guilt, I need not fear;
Nor would the thought distressing be,
Perhaps it next may toll for me.

Rather, my spirit would rejoice,
And long, and wish, to hear thy voice;
Glad when it bids me earth resign,
Secure of heav'n, if thou art mine.

Hymn 75
John Newton
Hope beyond the grave.

My soul, this curious house of clay,
Thy present frail abode;
Must quickly fall to worms a prey,
And thou return to GOD.

Canst thou, by faith, survey with joy
The change, before it come?
And say, "Let death this house destroy,
I have a heav'nly home!"

The Savior, whom I then shall see
With new admiring eyes,
Already has prepared for me,
A mansion in the skies.
2Cor 5:1

I feel this mud-walled cottage shake,
And long to see it fall;
That I my willing flight may take
To him who is my all.

Burdened and groaning, then no more,
My rescued soul shall sing,
As up the shining path I soar,
"Death, thou hast lost thy sting."

Dear Savior, help us now to seek,
And know thy grace's power;
That we may all this language speak,
Before the dying hour.

Hymn 76
John Newton
There the weary are at rest.

Courage, my soul! behold the prize
The Savior's love provides;
Eternal life beyond the skies,
For all whom here he guides.

The wicked cease from troubling there,
The weary are at rest;
Job 3:17
Sorrow and sin, and pain and care,
No more approach the blest.

A wicked world and wicked heart,
With Satan now are joined;
Each acts a too successful part
In harassing my mind.

In conflict with this threefold troop,
How weary, LORD, am I?
Did not thy promise bear me up,
My soul must faint and die.

But fighting in my Savior's strength,
Though mighty are my foes,
I shall a conqu'ror be at length,
O'er all that can oppose.

Then why, my soul, complain or fear?
The crown of glory see!
The more I toil and suffer here,
The sweeter rest will be.

Hymn 77
John Newton
The day of judgment.

Day of judgment, day of wonders!
Hark! the trumpet's aweful sound,
Louder than a thousand thunders,
Shakes the vast creation round!
How the summons wilt the sinner's heart confound!

See the Judge our nature wearing,
Clothed in majesty divine!
You who long for his appearing,
Then shall say, "This God is mine!"
Gracious Savior, own me in that day for thine!

At his call the dead awaken,
Rise to life from earth and sea;
All the pow'rs of nature shaken
By his look, prepares to flee:
Careless sinner, what will then become of thee!

Horrors, past imagination,
Will surprise your trembling heart,
When you hear your condemnation,
"Hence, accursed wretch, depart!
Thou, with Satan and his angels, have thy part!"

Satan, who now tries to please you,
Lest you timely warning take,
When that word is past, will seize you,
Plunge you in the burning lake:
Think, poor sinner, thy eternal all's at stake.

But to those who have confessed,
Loved and served the Lord below;
He will say, "Come near ye blessed;
See the kingdom I bestow:
You for ever shall my love and glory know."

Under sorrows and reproaches,
May this thought your courage raise!
Swiftly God's great day approaches,
Sighs shall then be changed to praise.
We shall triumph when the world is in a blaze.

Hymn 78
John Newton
The day of the Lord.[27]

God, with one piercing glance, looks through
Creation's wide extended frame;
The past and future in his view,
And days and ages are the same.
2Pet 2:8-10

Sinners, who dare provoke his face,
Who on his patience long presume,
And trifle out his day of grace,
Will find he has a day of doom.

As pangs the lab'ring woman feels,
Or as the thief, in midnight sleep;
So comes that day, for which the wheels
Of time, their ceaseless motion keep!

Hark! from the sky, the trump proclaims
Jesus; the Judge approaching nigh!
See, the creation wrapped in flames,
First kindled by his vengeful eye!

When thus the mountains melt like wax,
When earth, and air, and sea, shall burn;
When all the frame of nature breaks,
Poor sinner, whither wilt thou turn?

The puny works which feeble men
Now boast, or covet, or admire;
Their pomp, and arts, and treasures, then
Shall perish in one common fire.

LORD, fix our hearts and hopes above!
Since all below to ruin tends;
Here may we trust, obey, and love,
And there be found amongst thy friends.

Footnotes:
27. See also Book 2, Hymn 4

Hymn 79
John Newton
The great tribunal.
Rev 20:11,12

John in vision saw the day
When the Judge will hasten down;
Heav'n and earth shall flee away
From the terror of his frown:
Dead and living, small and great,
Raised from the earth and sea;
At his bar shall hear their fate,.
What will then become of me?

Can I bear his aweful looks?
Shall I stand in judgment then,
When I see the opened books,
Written by th' Almighty's pen?
If he to remembrance bring,
And expose to public view,
Every work and secret thing,
Ah, my soul, what canst thou do?

When the list shall be produced
Of the talents I enjoyed;
Means and mercies, how abused!
Time and strength, how misemployed!
Conscience then, compelled to read,
Must allow the charge is true;
Say, my soul, what canst thou plead
In that hour, what wilt thou do?

But the book of life I see,
May my name be written there!
Then from guilt and danger free,
Glad I'll meet him in the air:
That's the book I hope to plead,
'Tis the gospel opened wide;
Lord, I am a wretch indeed!
I have sinned, but thou hast died.
Rom 8:34

Now my soul knows what to do;
Thus I shall with boldness stand,
Numbered with the faithful few,

Olney Hymns
Owned and saved, at thy right hand:
If thou help a foolish worm
To believe thy promise now;
Justice will at last confirm
What thy mercy wrought below.

IV. CREATION

Hymn 80
John Newton
The old and new creation.

That was a wonder-working word
Which could the vast creation raise!
Angels, attendant on their LORD,
Job 38:7
Admired the plan, and sung his praise.

From what a dark and shapeless mass,
All nature sprang at his command!
Let there be light, and light there was,
And sun and stars, and sea and land.

With equal speed the earth and seas,
Their mighty Maker's voice obeyed;
He spake, and strait the plants and trees,
And birds, and beasts, and man were made.

But man, the lord and crown of all,
By sin his honor soon defaced;
His heart (how altered since the fall!)
Is dark, deformed, and void, and waste.

The new creation of the soul
Does now no less his pow'r display;
2Cor 4:6
Than when he formed the mighty whole,
And kindled darkness into day.

Though self-destroyed, O LORD, we are,
Yet let us feel what thou cast do;
Thy word the ruin can repair,
And all our hearts create anew.

Hymn 81
John Newton
The book of creation.

The book of nature open lies,
With much instruction stored;
But till the Lord anoints our eyes
We cannot read a word.

Philosophers have pored in vain,
And guessed, from age to age;
For reason's eye could ne'er attain
To understand a page.

Though to each star they give a name,
Its size and motions teach;
The truths which all the stars proclaim,
Their wisdom cannot reach.

With skill to measure earth and sea;
And weigh the subtle air;
They cannot, LORD, discover thee
Though present everywhere.

The knowledge of the saints excels
The wisdom of the schools;
To them his secrets God reveals,
Though men account them fools.

To them the sun and stars on high,
The flow'rs that paint the field,
Mt 6:26-28
And all the artless birds that fly,
Divine instruction yield.

The creatures on their senses press,
As witnesses to prove
Their Savior's pow'r, and faithfulness,
His providence and love.

Thus may we study nature's book
To make us wise indeed!
And pity those who only look
At what they cannot read.
Rom 1:20

Hymn 82
John Newton
The rainbow.

When the sun, with cheerful beams,
Smiles upon a low'ring sky;
Soon its aspect softened seems,
And a rainbow meets the eye:
While the sky remains serene,
This bright arch is never seen.

Thus the Lord's supporting pow'r
Brightest to his saints appears,
When affliction's threat'ning hour
Fills their sky with clouds and fears.
He can wonders then perform,
Paint a rainbow on the storm.
Gen 9:14

All their graces doubly shine
When their troubles press them fore;
And the promises divine
Give them joys unknown before:
As the colors of the bow,
To the cloud their brightness owe.

Favored John a rainbow saw
Rev 4:3
Circling round the throne above;
Hence the saints a pledge may draw
Of unchanging cov'nant love:
Clouds awhile may intervene,
But the bow will still be seen.

Hymn 83
John Newton
Thunder.

When a black overspreading cloud
Has dark'ned all the air;
And peals of thunder roaring loud
Proclaim the tempest near.

Then guilt and fear, the fruits of sin,
The sinner oft pursue;
A louder storm is heard within,
And conscience thunders too.

The law a fiery language speaks,
His danger he perceives;
Like Satan, who his ruin seeks,
He trembles and believes.

But when the sky serene appears,
And thunders roll no more;
He soon forgets his vows and fears,
Just as he did before.

But whither shall the sinner flee,
When nature's mighty frame,
The pond'rous earth, and air, and sea,
2Pet 3:10
Shall all dissolve in flame?

Amazing day! it comes apace!
The Judge is hasting down!
Will sinners bear to see his face,
Or stand before his frown?

Lord, let thy mercy find a way
To touch each stubborn heart
That they may never hear thee say,
"Ye cursed ones depart."

Believers, you may well rejoice!
The thunders loudest strains
Should be to you a welcome voice,
That tells you, "JESUS REIGNS!"

Hymn 84
John Newton
Lightning in the night.

A Glance from heav'n, with sweet effect,
Sometimes my pensive spirit cheers;
But, ere I can my thoughts collect,
As suddenly it disappears.

So lightning in the gloom of night,
Affords a momentary day;
Disclosing objects full in sight,
Which soon as seen, are snatched away.

Ah! what avail these pleasing scenes!
They do but aggravate my pain;
While darkness quickly intervenes,
And swallows up my joys again.

But shall I murmur at relief?
Though short, it was a precious view;
Sent to control my unbelief,
And prove that what I read is true.

The lightning's flash did not create
The op'ning prospect it revealed;
But only showed the real state
Of what the darkness had concealed.

Just so, we by a glimpse discern
The glorious things within the veil;
That when in darkness, we may learn
To live by faith, till light prevail.

The Lord's great day will soon advance,
Dispersing all the shades of night;
Then we no more shall need a glance,
But see by an eternal Light.

Hymn 85
John Newton
On the eclipse of the moon. July 30, 1776.

The moon in silver glory shone,
And not a cloud in sight;
When suddenly a shade begun
To intercept her light.

How fast across her orb it spread,
How fast her light withdrew!
A circle, tinged with languid red,
Was all appeared in view.

While many with unmeaning eye
Gaze on thy works in vain;
Assist me, LORD, that I may try
Instruction to obtain.

Fain would my thankful heart and lips
Unite in praise to thee;
And meditate on thy eclipse,
In sad Gethsemane.

Thy peoples guilt, a heavy load!
(When standing in their room)
Deprived thee of the light of God,
And filled thy soul with gloom.

How punctually eclipses move,
Obedient to thy will!
Thus shall thy faithfulness and love,
Thy promises fulfill.

Dark, like the moon without the sun,
I mourn thine absence, Lord!
For light or comfort I have none,
But what thy beams afford.

But lo! the hour draws near apace,
When changes shall be o'er;
Then I shall see thee face to face,
And be eclipsed no more.

Hymn 86
John Newton
Moon-light.

The moon has but a borrowed light,
A faint and feeble ray;
She owes her beauty to the night,
And hides herself by day.

No cheering warmth her beam conveys,
Though pleasing to behold;
We might upon her brightness gaze
Till we were starved with cold.

Just such is all the light to man
Which reason can impart;
It cannot show one object plain,
Nor warm the frozen heart.

Thus moonlight views of truths divine
To many fatal prove;
For what avail in gifts to shine,
1Cor 13:1
Without a spark of love?

The gospel, like the sun at noon,
Affords a glorious light;
Then fallen reason's boasted moon
Appears no longer bright.

And grace, not light alone, bestows,
But adds a quick'ing pow'r;
The desert blossoms like the rose,
Isa 35:1
And sin prevails no more.

Hymn 87
John Newton
The sea.[28]

If for a time the air be calm,
Serene and smooth the sea appears;
And shows no danger to alarm
The inexperienced landsman's fears.

But if the tempest once arise,
The faithless water swells and raves;
Its billows, foaming to the skies,
Disclose a thousand threat'ning graves.

My untried heart thus seemed to me,
(So little of myself I knew)
Smooth as the calm unruffled sea,
But ah! it proved as treach'rous too!

The peace, of which I had a taste,
When Jesus first his love revealed
I fondly hoped would always last,
Because my foes were then concealed.

But when I felt the tempter's pow'r
Rouse my corruptions from their sleep;
I trembled at the stormy hour,
And saw the horrors of the deep.

Now, on presumption's billows borne,
My spirit seemed the LORD to dare;
Now, quick as thought, a sudden turn
Plunged me in gulfs of black despair.

LORD, save me, or I sink, I prayed,
He heard, and bid the tempest cease;
The angry waves his word obeyed,
And all my fears were hushed to peace.

The peace is his, and not my own,
My heart (no better than before)
Is still to dreadful changes prone,
Then let me never trust it more.

Footnotes:
28. See also Book 1, Hymn 115

Hymn 88
John Newton
The flood.

Though small the drops of falling rain,
If one be singly viewed;
Collected, they o'erspread the plain,
And form a mighty flood.

The house it meets with in its course,
Should not he built on clay;
Lest, with a wild resistless force,
It sweep the whole away.

Though for awhile it seemed secure,
It will not bear the shock;
Unless it has foundations sure,
And stands upon a rock.

Thus sinners think their evil deeds,
Like drops of rain, are small;
But it the pow'r of thought exceeds,
To count the sum of all.

One sin can raise, though small it seems,
A flood to drown the soul;
What then, when countless million streams
Shall join, to swell the whole.

Yet, while they think the weather fair,
If warned, they smile or frown;
But they will tremble and despair,
When the fierce flood comes down!

O! then on Jesus ground your hope,
That stone in Zion laid;
Mt 7:24 1Pet 2:6
Lest your poor building quickly drop,
With ruin, on your head.

Hymn 89
John Newton
The thaw.

The ice and snow we lately saw,
Which covered all the ground;
Are melted soon before the thaw,
And can no more be found.

Could all the art of man suffice
To move away the snow,
To clear the rivers from the ice,
Or make the waters flow?

No, 'tis the work of GOD alone;
An emblem of the pow'r
By which he melts the heart of stone,
In his appointed hour.

All outward means, till he appears,
Will ineffectual prove;
Though much the sinner sees and hears,
He cannot learn to love.

But let the stoutest sinner feel
The soft'ning warmth of grace;
Though hard as ice, or rocks, or steel,
His heart dissolves apace.

Seeing the blood which JESUS spilt,
To save his soul from woe,
His hatred, unbelief, and guilt,
All melt away like snow.

Jesus, we in thy name entreat,
Reveal thy gracious arm;
And grant thy Spirit's kindly heat,
Our frozen hearts to warm.

Hymn 90
John Newton
The Lodestone.

As needles point towards the pole,
When touched by the magnetic stone;
So faith in JESUS, gives the soul
A tendency before unknown.

Till then, by blinded passions led,
In search of fancied good we range;
The paths of disappointment tread,
To nothing fixed, but love of change.

But when the Holy Ghost imparts
A knowledge of the Savior's love;
Our wand'ring, weary, restless hearts,
Are fixed at once, no more to move.

Now a new principle takes place,
Which guides and animates the will;
This love, another name for grace,
Constrains to good, and bars from ill.

By love's sure light we soon perceive
Our noblest bliss, and proper end;
And gladly every idol leave,
To love and serve our Lord and Friend.

Thus borne along by faith and hope,
We feel the Savior's words are true;
"And I, if I be lifted up,
Jn 7:32
Will draw the sinner upward too."

Hymn 91
John Newton
The spider and bee.

On the same flow'r we often see
The loathsome spider and the bee;
But what they get by working there,
Is different as their natures are.

The bee a sweet reward obtains,
And honey well repays his pains;
Home to the hive he bears the store,
And then returns in quest of more.

But no sweet flow'rs that grace the field,
Can honey to the spider yield;
A cobweb all that he can spin,
And poison all he stores within.

Thus in that sacred field the word,
With flow'rs of GOD'S own planting stored,
Like bees his children feed and thrive,
And bring home honey to the hive.

There, spider-like, the wicked come,
And seem to taste the same perfume,
But the vile venom of their hearts,
To poison all their food converts.

From the same truths believers prize.
They weave vain refuges of lies;
And from the promise licence draw,
To trifle with the holy law!

LORD, shall thy word of life and love,
The means of death to numbers prove!
Unless thy grace our hearts renew, [29]
We sink to hell, with heav'n in view.

Footnotes:
29. See also Book 3, Hymn 71

Hymn 92
John Newton
The bee saved from the spider.

The subtle spider often weaves
His unsuspected snares,
Among the balmy flow'rs and leaves,
To which the bee repairs.

When in his web he sees one hang,
With a malicious joy,
He darts upon it with his fang,
To poison and destroy.

How welcome then, some pitying friend,
To save the threatened bee!
The spider's treach'rous web to rend,
And set the captive free!

My soul has been in such a case,
When first I knew the LORD,
I hasted to the means of grace,
Where sweets I knew were stored.

Little I thought of danger near,
That soon my joys would ebb;
But ah! I met a spider there,
Who caught me in his web.

Then Satan raised his pois'nous sting,
And aimed his blows at me;
While I, poor helpless trembling thing,
Could neither fight nor flee.

But O! the Savior's pitying eye
Relieved me from despair;
He saw me at the point to die
And broke the fatal snare.

My case his heedless saints should warn,
Or cheer them if afraid;
May you from me your danger learn,
And where to look for aid.

Hymn 93
John Newton
The tamed lion.

A Lion, though by nature wild,
The art of man can tame;
He stands before his keeper, mild,
And gentle as a lamb.

He watches, with submissive eye,
The hand that gives him food;
As if he meant to testify
A sense of gratitude.

But man himself, who thus subdues
The fiercest beasts of prey;
A nature, more unfeeling shows,
And far more fierce than they.

Though by the LORD preserved and fed,
He proves rebellious still;
And while he eats his Maker's bread,
Resists his holy will.

Alike in vain, of grace that saves,
Or threat'ning law he hears;
The savage scorns, blasphemes, and raves,
But neither loves nor fears.

O Savior! how thy wondrous pow'r
By angels is proclaimed!
When in thine own appointed hour,
They see this lion tamed.

The love thy bleeding cross displays,
The hardest heart subdues;
Here furious lions while they gaze,
Their rage and fierceness lose.
Isa 11:6

Yet are we but renewed in part,
The lion still remains;
LORD, drive him wholly from my heart,
Or keep him fast in chains.

Hymn 94
John Newton
Sheep.

The Savior calls his people sheep,
And bids them on his love rely,
For he alone their souls can keep,
And he alone their wants supply.

The bull can fight, the hare can flee,
The ant, in summer, food prepare;
But helpless sheep, and such are we,
Depend upon the Shepherd's care.

JEHOVAH is our Shepherd's name,
Ps 23:1
Then what have we, though weak, to fear?
Our sin and folly we proclaim,
If we despond while he is near.

When Satan threatens to devour,
When troubles press on every side;
Think of our Shepherd's care and pow'r,
He can defend, he will provide.

See the rich pastures of his grace,
Where, in full streams, salvation flows!
There he appoints our resting place,
And we may feed, secure from foes.

There, 'midst the flock the Shepherd dwells,
The sheep around in safety lie;
The wolf, in vain, with malice swells,
For he protects them with his eye.
Mic 5:4

Dear LORD, if I am one of thine,
From anxious thoughts I would be free;
To trust, and love, and praise, is mine,
The care of all belongs to thee.

Hymn 95
John Newton
The garden.

A Garden contemplation suits,
And may instruction yield,
Sweeter than all the flow'rs and fruits
With which the spot is filled.

Eden was Adam's dwelling place,
While blest with innocence;
But sin o'erwhelmed him with disgrace,
And drove the rebel thence.

Oft as the garden-walk we tread,
We should bemoan his fall;
The trespass of our legal head
In ruin plunged us all.

The garden of Gethsemane,
The second Adam saw,
Oppressed with woe, to set us free
From the avenging law.

How stupid we, who can forget,
With gardens in our sight,
His agonies and bloody sweat,
In that tremendous night

His church as a fair garden stands,
Which walls of love enclose;
Each tree is planted by his hand,
Isa 61:3
And by his blessing grows.

Believing hearts are gardens too,
For grace has sown its seeds;
Where once, by nature, nothing grew
But thorns and worthless weeds.

Such themes to those who JESUS love,
May constant joys afford;
And make a barren desert prove
The garden of the LORD.

Hymn 96
John Newton
For a garden-seat, or summer-house.

A Shelter from the rain or wind,
Isa 32:2
A shade from scorching heats
A resting place you here may find,
To ease your weary feet.

Enter but with a serious thought,
Consider who is near
This is a consecrated spot,
The Lord is present here!

A question of the utmost weight,
While reading, meets your eye;
May conscience witness to your state,
And give a true reply!

Is Jesus to your heart revealed,
As full of truth and grace?
And is his name your hope and shield,
Your rest and hiding place?

If so, for all events prepared,
Whatever storms may rise,
He, whom you love, wilt safely guard,
And guide you to the skies.

No burning sun, or storm, or rain,
Will there your peace annoy;
No sin, temptation, grief, or pain,
Intrude to damp your joy.

But if his name you have not known,
Oh, seek him while you may!
Lest you should meet his aweful frown,
In that approaching day.

When the avenging Judge you see,
With terrors on his brow;
Where can you hide, or whither flee,
If you reject him now?

Hymn 97
John Newton
The creatures in the LORD's hands.

The water stood like walls of brass,
To let the sons of Israel pass;
Ex 14:22
And from the rock in rivers burst
Num 20:11
At Moses' prayer to quench their thirst.

The fire restrained by God's commands,
Could only burn his people's bands;
Dan 3:27
Too faint, when he was with them there,
To singe their garments or their hair.

At Daniel's feet the lions lay
Dan 4:23
Like harmless lambs, nor touched their prey;
And ravens, which on carrion fed,
Procured Elijah flesh and bread.

Thus creatures only can fulfill
Their great Creator's holy will;
And when his servants need their aid,
His purposes must be obeyed.

So if his blessing he refuse,
Their pow'r to help they quickly lose,
Sure as on creatures we depend,
Our hopes in disappointment end.

Then let us trust the LORD alone,
And creature-confidence disown;
Nor if they threaten need we fear,
They cannot hurt if he be near.

If instruments of pain they prove,
Still they are guided by his love;
As lancets by the surgeon's skill,
Which wound to cure, and not to kill.

Hymn 98
John Newton
On dreaming.

When slumber seals our weary eyes,
The busy fancy wakeful keeps;
The scenes which then before us rise,
Prove, something in us never sleeps.

As in another world we seem,
A new creation of our own;
All appears real, though a dream,
And all familiar, though unknown.

Sometimes the mind beholds again
The past days business in review;
Resumes the pleasure or the pain,
And sometimes all we meet is new.

What schemes we form, what pains we take!
We fight, we run, we fly, we fall;
But all is ended when we wake,
We scarcely then a trace recall.

But though our dreams are often wild,
Like clouds before the driving storm;
Yet some important may be styled,
Sent to admonish or inform.

What mighty agents have access,
What friends from heav'n, or foes from hell,
Our minds to comfort or distress,
When we are sleeping, who can tell?

One thing, at least, and 'tis enough,
We learn from this surprising fact;
Our dreams afford sufficient proof,
The soul, without the flesh, can act.

This life, which mortals so esteem,
That many choose it for their all,
They will confess, was but a dream,
Isa 29:8
When wakened by death's awful call.

Hymn 99

John Newton
The world.

See, the world for youth prepares,
Harlot like, her gaudy snares!
Pleasures round her seem to wait,
But 'tis all a painted cheat.

Rash and unsuspecting youth
Thinks to find thee always smooth,
Always kind, till better taught,
By experience dearly bought.

So the calm, but faithless sea,
(Lively emblem, world, of thee)
Tempts the shepherd from the shore,
Foreign regions to explore.

While no wrinkled wave is seen,
While the sky remains serene;
Filled with hopes, and golden schemes,
Of a storm he little dreams.

But ere long the tempest raves,
Then he trembles at the waves;
Wishes then he had been wise,
But too late-he sinks and dies.

Hapless thus, are they, vain world,
Soon on rocks of ruin hurled;
Who admiring thee, untried,
Court thy pleasure, wealth, or pride.

Such a shipwreck had been mine,
Had not JESUS (Name Divine!)
Saved me with a mighty hand,
And restored my soul to land.

Now, with gratitude I raise
Ebenezers to his praise;
Now my rash pursuits are o'er,
I can trust thee, world, no more.

Hymn 100
John Newton
The enchantment dissolved.

Blinded in youth by Satan's arts,
The world to our unpracticed hearts,
A flatt'ring prospect bows;
Our fancy forms a thousand schemes,
Of gay delights, and golden dreams,
And undisturbed repose.

So in the desert's dreary waste,
By magic pow'r produced in haste,
(As ancient fables say)
Castles, and groves, and music sweet,
The senses of the trav'ller meet,
And stop him in his way.

But while he listens with surprise,
The charm dissolves, the vision dies,
'Twas but enchanted ground;
Thus if the Lord our spirits touch,
The world, which promised us so much,
A wilderness is found.

At first we start, and feel distressed,
Convinced we never can have rest,
In such a wretched place;
But he whose mercy breaks the charm,
Reveals his own almighty arm,
And bids us seek his face.

Then we begin to live indeed,
When from our sin and bondage freed,
By this beloved Friend;
We follow him from day to day,
Assured of grace through all the way,
And glory at the end.

John Newton

BOOK III

On the Rise, Progress, Changes, and Comforts of the Spiritual Life.
    (Under the following Heads)
    I. Solemn Addresses to Sinners.
    II. Seeking, Pleading, Hoping.
    III. Conflict.
    IV. Comfort.
    V. Dedication and Surrender.
    VI. Cautions.
    VII. Praise.
    VIII. Short Hymns.
    Before Sermon.
    After Sermon.
    Gloria Patri.

I. Solemn Addresses to Sinners

Hymn 1
John Newton
10,10,11,11

No words can declare,
No fancy can paint,
What rage and despair,
What hopeless complaint,
Fill Satan's dark dwelling,
The prison beneath;
What weeping and yelling,
And gnashing of teeth!

Yet sinners will choose
This dreadful abode,
Each madly persues
The dangerous road;
Though God give them warning
They onward will go,
They answer with scorning,
And onward do go.

How sad to behold
The rich and the poor,
The young and the old,

Olney Hymns

All blindly secure!
All posting to ruin,
Refusing to stop;
Ah! think what you're doing,
While yet there is hope!

How weak is your hand
To fight with the LORD!
How can you withstand
The edge of his sword?
What hope of escaping
For those who oppose,
When hell is wide gaping
To swallow his foes?

How oft have you dared
The Lord to his face!
Yet still you are spared
To hear of his grace;
O pray for repentance
And life-giving faith,
Before the just sentence
Consign you to death.

It is not too late
To JESUS to flee,
His mercy is great,
His pardon is free;
His blood has such virtue
For all that believe,
That nothing can hurt you,
If him you receive.

Hymn 2
John Newton
Alarm.

Stop, poor sinner! stop and think
Before you farther go!
Will you sport upon the brink
Of everlasting woe?
Once again I charge you, stop!
For, unless you warning take,
Ere you are aware, you drop
Into the burning lake!

Say, have you an arm like God,
That you his will oppose?
Fear you not that iron rod
With which he breaks his foes?
Can you stand in that dread day,
When he judgment shall proclaim,
And the earth shall melt away
Like wax before the flame?

Palefaced death will quickly come
To drag you to his bar;
Then to hear your awful doom
Will fill you with despair:
All your sins will round you crowd,
Sins of a blood-crimson dye;
Each for vengeance crying loud,
And what can you reply?

Though your heart be made of steel,
Your forehead lined with brass,
GOD at length will make you feel,
He will not let you pass:
Sinners then in vain will call,
(Though they now despise his grace)
Rocks and mountains on us fall,
Rev 6:16
And hide us from his face!

But as yet there is a hope
You may his mercy know;
Though his arm is lifted up,
He still forbears the blow:

Olney Hymns
'Twas for sinners Jesus died,
Sinners he invites to come;
None who come shall be denied,
He says, "There still is room."
Lk 14:22

Hymn 3
John Newton
We were once as you are.

Shall men pretend to pleasure
Who never knew the LORD?
Can all the worldling's treasure
True peace of mind afford?
They shall obtain this jewel
In what their hearts desire,
When they by adding fuel
Can quench the flame of fire.

Till you can bid the ocean,
When furious tempests roar,
Isa 57:20,21
Forget its wonted motion,
And rage, and swell, no more:
In vain your expectation
To find content in sin;
Or freedom from vexation,
While passions reign within.

Come, turn your thoughts to JESUS,
If you would good possess;
'Tis he alone that frees us
From guilt, and from distress:
When he, by faith, is present,
The sinner's troubles cease;
His ways are truly pleasant,
Pr 3:17
And all his paths are peace.

Our time in sin we wasted,
And fed upon the wind;
Until his love we tasted,
No comfort could we find:
But now we stand to witness
His pow'r and grace to you;
May you perceive its fitness,
And call upon him too!

Our pleasure and our duty,
Though opposite before;
Since we have seen his beauty,

Olney Hymns
Are joined to part no more:
It is our highest pleasure,
No less than duty's call;
To love him beyond measure,
And serve him with our all.

John Newton

Hymn 4
John Newton
Prepare to meet God.

Sinner, art thou still secure?
Wilt thou still refuse to pray?
Can thy heart or hands endure
In the LORD'S avenging day?
See, his mighty arm is bared!
Aweful terrors clothe his brow!
For his judgment stand prepared,
Thou must either break or bow.

At his presence nature shakes,
Earth affrighted hastes to flee;
Solid mountains melt like wax,
What will then become of thee?
Who his advent may abide?
You that glory in your shame,
Will you find a place to hide
When the world is wrapped in flame?

Then the rich, the great, the wise,
Trembling, guilty, self-condemned;
Must behold the wrathful eyes
Of the Judge they once blasphemed:
Where are now their haughty looks?
O, their horror and despair!
When they see the opened books
And their dreadful sentence hear!

LORD prepare us by thy grace!
Soon we must resign our breath;
And our souls be called, to pass
Through the iron gate of death
Let us now our day improve,
Listen to the gospel voice;
Seek the things that are above,
Scorn the world's pretended joys.

O! when flesh and heart shall fail,
Let thy love our spirits cheer;
Strengthened thus, we shall prevail

Olney Hymns
Over Satan, sin, and fear:
Trusting in thy precious name,
May we thus our journey end;
Then our foes hall lose their aim,
And the Judge will be our Friend.

Hymn 5
John Newton
Invitation.

Sinner, hear the Savior's call,
He now is passing by;
He has seen thy grievous thrall,
And heard thy mournful cry.
He has pardons to impart,
Grace to save thee from thy fears,
See the love that fills his heart,
And wipe away thy tears.

Why art thou afraid to come
And tell him all thy case?
He will not pronounce thy doom,
Nor frown thee from his face:
Wilt thou fear EMMANUEL?
Wilt thou dread the Lamb of God,
Who, to save thy soul from hell,
Has shed his precious blood?

Think, how on the cross he hung
Pierced with a thousand wounds!
Hark, from each as with a tongue
The voice of pardon sounds!
See, from all his bursting veins,
Blood, of wondrous virtue, flow!
Shed to wash away thy stains,
And ransom thee from woe.

Though his majesty be great,
His mercy is no less;
Though he thy transgressions hate,
He feels for thy distress:
By himself the LORD has sworn,
He delights not in thy death;
Ezek 33:11
But invites thee to return,
That thou mayst live by faith.

Raise thy downcast eyes, and see
What throngs his throne surround!
These, though sinners once like thee,
Have full salvation found:

Olney Hymns
Yield not then to unbelief!
While he says, "There yet is room;"
Though of sinners thou art chief,
Since Jesus calls thee, come.

II. Seeking, Pleading, and Hoping

Hymn 6
John Newton
The hardened sinner.

Ah, what can I do,
Or where be secure!
If justice pursue
What heart can endure!
When GOD speaks in thunder,
And makes himself known,
The heart breaks asunder
Though hard as a stone.

With terror I read
My sins heavy score,
The numbers exceed
The sands on the shore;
Guilt makes me unable
To stand or to flee,
So Cain murdered Abel,
And trembled like me.

Each sin, like his blood,
With a terrible cry,
Calls loudly on God
To strike from on high:
Nor can my repentance
Extorted by fear,
Reverse the just sentence,
'Tis just though severe.

The case is too plain,
I have my own choice;
Again, and again
I slighted his voice;
His warnings neglected,
His patience abused,
His gospel rejected,
His mercy refused.

And must I then go,
Forever to dwell

Olney Hymns
In torments and woe
With devils in hell?
Oh where is the Savior
I scorned in times past?
His word in my favor
Would save me at last.

Lord JESUS, on thee
I venture to call,
Oh look upon me
The vilest of all!
For whom didst thou languish,
And bleed on the tree?
Oh pity my anguish,
And say, "'Twas for thee."

A case such as mine
Will honor thy pow'r;
All hell will repine,
All heav'n will adore;
If in condemnation
Strict justice takes place,
It shines in salvation
More glorious through grace.

Hymn 7
John Newton
Behold I am vile!

O LORD, how vile am I,
Unholy, and unclean!
How can I dare to venture nigh
With such a load of sin?

Is this polluted heart
A dwelling fit for thee?
Swarming, alas! I in every part,
What evils do I see!

If I attempt to pray,
And lisp thy holy name;
My thoughts are hurried soon away,
I know not where I am.

If in thy word I look,
Such darkness fills my mind,
I only read a sealed book,
But no relief can find.

Thy gospel oft I hear,
But hear it still in vain;
Without desire, or love, or fear,
I like a stone remain.

Myself can hardly bear
This wretched heart of mine;
How hateful then must it appear
To those pure eyes of thine?

And must I then indeed
Sink in despair and die?
Fain would I hope that thou didst bleed
For such a wretch as I.

That blood which thou hast spilt;
That grace which is thine own;
Can cleanse the vilest sinner's guilt,
And soften hearts of stone.

Olney Hymns
Low at thy feet I bow,
O pity and forgive;
Here will I lie and wait, till thou
Shalt bid me rise and live.

Hymn 8
William Cowper
The shining Light.

My former hopes are dead,
My terror now begins;
I feel, alas! that I am dead
In trespasses and sins.

Ah, whither shall I fly?
I hear the thunder roar
The law proclaims destruction nigh,
And vengeance at the door.

When I review my ways,
I dread impending doom;
But sure, a friendly whisper says,
"Flee from the wrath to come."

I see, or think I see,
A glimm'ring from afar;
A beam of day that shines for me,
To save me from despair.

Fore-runner of the sun,
Ps 130:6
It marks the Pilgrim's way;
I'll gaze upon it while I run,
And watch the rising day.

Hymn 9
John Newton
Encouragement.

My soul is beset
With grief and dismay,
I owe a vast debt
And nothing can pay:
I must go to prison,
Unless that dear Lord,
Who died and is risen,
His pity afford.

The death that he died,
The blood that he spilt,
To sinners applied,
Discharge from all guilt:
This great Intercessor
Can give, if he please,
The vilest transgressor
Immediate release.

When nailed to the tree,
He answered the prayer
Of one, who like me,
Was nigh to despair;
Lk 23:43
He did not upbraid him
With all he had done,
But instantly made him,
A saint and a son.

The jailor, I read,
A pardon received;
Acts 16:31
And how was he freed?
He only believed:
His case mine resembled,
Like me he was foul,
Like me too he trembled,
Rut faith made him whole.

Though Saul in his youth,
To madness enraged,
Against the Lord's truth,

John Newton

And people, engaged;
Yet Jesus, the Savior,
Whom long he reviled;
1Tim 1:16
Received him to favor
And made him a child.

A foe to all good,
In wickedness skilled,
Manasseh, with blood,
Jerusalem filled;
2Chr 33:12,13
In evil long hardened,
The LORD he defied,
Yet he too was pardoned,
When mercy he cried.

Of sinners the chief,
And viler than all,
The jailor or thief,
Manasseh or Saul:
Since they were forgiven
Why should I despair,
While CHRIST is in heaven,
And still answers prayer?

Hymn 10
William Cowper
The waiting soul

Breathe from the gentle South, O LORD,
And cheer me from the North;
Blow on the treasures of thy word,
And call the spices forth!

I wish, thou know'st, to be resigned,
And wait with patient hope;
But hope delayed fatigues the mind,
And drinks the spirit up.

Help me to reach the distant goal;
Confirm my feeble knee;
Pity the sickness of a soul
That faints for love of thee.

Cold as I feel this heart of mine,
Yet since I feel it so;
It yields some hope of life divine
Within, however low.

I seem forsaken and alone,
I hear the lion roar;
And every door is shut but one,
And that is mercy's door.

There, till the dear Deliv'rer come,
I'll wait with humble prayer
And when he calls his exile home,
The Lord, shall find me there.

Hymn 11
John Newton
The effort.

Cheer up, my soul, there is a mercy-seat
Sprinkled with blood, where JESUS answers prayer;
There humbly cast thyself, beneath his feet,
For never needy sinner perished there.

Lord, I am come! thy promise is my plea,
Without thy word I durst not venture nigh;
But thou hast called the burdened soul to thee,
A weary burdened soul, O Lord, am I!

Bowed down beneath a heavy load of sin,
By Satan's fierce temptations sorely pressed,
Beset without, and full of fears within,
Trembling and faint I come to thee for rest.

Be thou my refuge, Lord, my hiding-place,
I know no force can tear me from thy side;
Unmoved I then may all accusers face,
And answer every charge, with, "JESUS died."

Yes, thou didst weep, and bleed, and groan, and die,
Well hast thou known what fierce temptations mean;.
Such was thy love, and now, enthroned on high,
The same compassions in thy bosom reign.

Lord give me faith--he hears--what grace is this!
Dry up thy tears, my soul, and cease to grieve:
He shows me what he did, and who he is,
I must, I will, I can, I do believe.

Hymn 12
John Newton
The effort.

Approach, my soul, the mercy-seat
Where JESUS answers prayer;
There humbly fall before his feet,
For none can perish there.

Thy promise is my only plea,
With this I venture nigh;
Thou callest burdened souls to thee,
And such, O LORD, am I.

Bowed down beneath a load of sin,
By Satan sorely pressed;
By war without, and fears within,
I come to thee for rest.

Be thou my shield and hiding-place!
That, sheltered near thy side,
I may my fierce accuser face,
And tell him, "Thou hast died."

Oh wondrous love! to bleed and die,
To bear the cross and shame;
That guilty sinners, such as I,
Might plead thy gracious name.

"Poor tempest-tossed soul, be still,
My promised grace receive;"
'Tis JESUS speaks--I must, I will,
I can, I do believe.

Hymn 13
William Cowper
Seeking the beloved.

To those who know the LORD I speak,
Is my beloved near?
The bridegroom of my soul I seek,
O! when will he appear!

Though once a man of grief and shame,
Yet now he fills a throne;
And bears the greatest, sweetest name,
That earth or heav'n have known.

Grace flies before, and love attends
His steps where'er be goes;
Though none can see him but his friends,
And they were once his foes.

He speaks--obedient to his call
Our warm affections move;
Did he but shine alike on all,
Then all alike would love.

Then love in every heart would reign,
And war would cease to roar;
And cruel, and blood-thirsty men,
Would thirst for blood no more.

Such JESUS is, and such his grace,
Oh may he shine on you!
SS 5:8
And tell him, when you see his face,
I long to see him too.

Hymn 14
John Newton
Rest for weary souls.

Does the gospel-word proclaim
Rest, for those who weary be?
Mt 11:28
Then, my soul, put in thy claim,
Sure that promise speaks to thee:
Marks of grace I cannot show,
All polluted is my best;
Yet I weary am I know,
And the weary long for rest.

Burdened with a load of sin,
Harassed with tormenting doubt,
Hourly conflicts from within,
Hourly crosses from without:
All my little strength is gone,
Sink I must without supply;
Sure upon the earth is none
Can more weary be than I.

In the ark, the weary dove
Gen 8:9
Found a welcome resting-place;
Thus my spirit longs to prove
Rest in CHRIST, the ark of grace:
Tempest-tossed I long have been,
And the flood increases fast;
Open, LORD, and take me in,
Till the storm be overpast.

Safely lodged within thy breast,
What a wondrous change I find!
Now I know thy promised rest
Can compose a troubled mind
You that weary are like me,
Hearken to the gospel call;
To the ark for refuge flee,
JESUS will receive you all!

III. CONFLICT

Hymn 15
William Cowper
Light shining out of darkness.

God moves in a mysterious way,
His wonders to perform;
He plants his footsteps in the sea,
And rides upon the storm.

Deep in unfathomable mines
Of never failing skill
He treasures up his bright designs,
And works his sovereign will.

Ye fearful saints fresh courage take,
The clouds ye so much dread
Are big with mercy, and shall break
In blessings on your head.

Judge not the LORD by feeble sense,
But trust him for his grace;
Behind a frowning providence,
He hides a smiling face.

His purposes will ripen fast,
Unfolding every hour;
The bud may have a bitter taste,
But sweet will be the flow'r.

Blind unbelief is sure to err,
Jn 8:7
And scan his work in vain;
GOD is his own interpreter,
And he will make it plain.

Hymn 16
William Cowper
Welcome cross.

'Tis my happiness below
Not to live without the cross;
But the Savior's pow'r to know,
Sanctifying every loss:
Trials must and will befall;
But with humble faith to see
Love inscribed upon them all,
This is happiness to me.

God, in Israel, sows the seeds
Of affliction, pain, and toil;
These spring up, and choke the weeds
Which would else o'erspread the soil:
Trials make the promise sweet,
Trials give hew life to prayer;
Trials bring me to his feet,
Lay me low, and keep me there.

Did I meet no trials here,
No chastisement by the way;
Might I not, with reason, fear
I should prove a cast-away:
Bastards may escape the rod,
Heb 12:8
Sunk in earthly, vain delight;
But the true-born child of GOD,
Must not, would not, if he might.

Hymn 17
William Cowper
Afflictions sanctified by the word.

O How I love thy holy word,
Thy gracious covenant, O LORD!
It guides me in the peaceful way,
I think upon it all the day.

What are the mines of shining wealth,
The strength of youth, the bloom of health!
What are all joys compared with those
Thine everlasting word bestows!

Long unafflicted, undismayed,
In pleasures path secure I strayed;
Thou mad'st me feel thy chast'ning rod,
Ps 119:71
And strait I turned unto my GOD.

What though it pierced my fainting heart,
I bless thine hand that caused the smart;
It taught my tears awhile to flow,
But saved me from eternal woe.

O! hadst thou left me unchastised,
Thy precept I had still despised;
And still the snare in secret laid,
Had my unwary feet betrayed.

I love thee therefore O my God,
And breathe towards thy dear abode;
Where in thy presence fully blest,
Thy chosen saints for ever rest.

Hymn 18
William Cowper
Temptation.

The billows swell the winds are high,
Clouds overcast my wintry sky;
Out of the depths to thee I call,
My fears are great, my strength is small.

O Lord, the pilot's part perform,
And guide and guard me through the storm;
Defend me from each threat'ning ill,
Control the waves, say, "Peace, be still!"

Amidst the roaring of the sea,
My soul still hangs her hope on thee;
Thy constant love, thy faithful care,
Is all that saves me from despair.

Dangers of every shape and name
Attend the follow'rs of the Lamb,
Who leave the world's deceitful shore,
And leave it to return no more.

Though tempest-tossed and half a wreck,
My Savior through the floods I seek;
Let neither winds nor stormy main,
Force back my shattered bark again.

Hymn 19
William Cowper
Looking upwards in a storm.

God of my life, to thee I call,
Afflicted at thy feet I fall;
Ps 69:15
When the great water-floods prevail,
Leave not my trembling heart to fail!

Friend of the friendless, and the saint!
Where should I lodge my deep complaint?
Where but with thee, whose open door,
Invites the helpless and the poor!

Did ever mourner plead with thee,
And thou refuse that mourner's plea?
Does not the word still fixed remain,
That none shall seek thy face in vain?

That were a grief I could not bear,
Didst thou not hear and answer prayer;
But a prayer-hearing, answ'ring God,
Supports me under every load.

Fair is the lot that's cast for me!
I have an advocate with thee;
They whom the world caresses most,
Have no such privilege to boast.

Poor though I am, despised, forgot,
Ps 60:17
Yet God, my God, forgets me not;
And he is safe and must succeed,
For whom the LORD vouchsafes to plead.

Hymn 20
William Cowper
The valley of the shadow of death.

My soul is sad and much dismayed;
See, LORD, what legions of my foes,
With fierce Apollyon at their head,
My heav'nly pilgrimage oppose!

See, from the over-burning lake
How like a smoky cloud they rise!
With horrid blasts my soul they shake,
With storms of blasphemies and lies.

Their fiery arrows reach the mark,
Eph 6:16
My throbbing heart with anguish tear;
Each lights upon a kindred spark,
And finds abundant fuel there.

I hate the thought that wrongs the LORD;
O, I would drive it from my breast,
With thy own sharp two-edged sword,
Far as the east is from the west!

Come then, and chase the cruel host,
Heal the deep wounds I have received!
Nor let the pow'rs of darkness boast
That I am foiled, and thou art grieved!

Hymn 21
John Newton
The storm hushed.

'Tis past--the dreadful stormy night
Is gone, with all its fears!
And now I see returning light,
The Lord, my Sun, appears.

The tempter, who but lately said,
I soon shall be his prey;
Has heard my Savior's voice and fled
With shame and grief away.

Ah, LORD, since thou didst hide thy face,
What has my soul endured?
But now 'tis past, I feel thy grace,
And all my wounds are cured!

O wondrous change! but just before
Despair beset me round;
I heard the lion's horrid roar,
And trembled at the sound.

Before corruption, guilt and fear,
My comfort blasted fell;
And unbelief discovered near
The dreadful depths of hell.

But JESUS pitied my distress,
He heard my feeble cry;
Revealed his blood and righteousness,
And brought salvation nigh.

Beneath the banner of his love,
I now secure remain;
The tempter frets, but dares not move
To break my peace again.

LORD, since thou thus hast broke my bands,
And set the captive free;
I would devote my tongue, my hands,
My heart, my all to thee.

Hymn 22
John Newton
Help in time of Need.

Unless the LORD had been my stay
(With trembling joy my soul may say)
My cruel foe had gained his end:
But he appeared for my relief,
And Satan sees, with shame and grief,
That I have an almighty Friend.

O, 'twas a dark and trying hour,
When harassed by the tempter's pow'r,
I felt my strongest hopes decline!
You only who have known his arts,
You only who have felt his darts,
Can pity such a case as mine.

Loud in my ears a charge he read,
(My conscience witnessed all he said)
My long black list of outward sin;
Then bringing forth my heart to view,
Too well what's hidden there he knew,
He showed me ten-times worse within.

'Tis all too true, my soul replied,
But I remember Jesus died,
And now he fills a throne of grace;
I'll go, as I have done before,
His mercy I may still implore,
I have his promise, "Seek my face."

But, as when sudden fogs arise,
The trees and hills, the sun and skies,
Are all at once concealed from view;
So clouds of horror, black as night,
By Satan raised, hid from my sight,
The throne of grace and promise too.

Then, while beset with guilt and fear,
He tried to urge me to despair,
He tried, and he almost prevailed;
But JESUS, by a heav'nly ray,
Drove clouds, and guilt, and fear away,
And all the tempter's malice failed.

Hymn 23
William Cowper
Peace after a storm.

When darkness long has veiled my mind,
And smiling day once more appears;
Then, my Redeemer, then I find
The folly of my doubts and fears.

Strait I upbraid my wand'ring heart,
And blush that I should ever be
Thus prone to act so base a part,
Or harbor one hard thought of thee!

O! let me then at length be taught
What I am still so slow to learn;
That God is love, and changes not,
Nor knows the shadow of a turn,

Sweet truth, and easy to repeat!
But when my faith is sharply tried,
I find myself a learner yet,
Unskillful, weak, and apt to slide.

But, O my LORD, one look from thee
Subdues the disobedient will;
Drives doubt and discontent away,
And thy rebellious worm is still.

Thou art as ready to forgive,
As I am ready to repine;
Thou, therefore, all the praise receive,
Be shame, and self-abhorrence, mine.

Hymn 24
William Cowper
Mourning and longing.

The Savior hides his face!
My spirit thirsts to prove
Renewed supplies of pard'ning grace,
And never-fading love.

The favored souls who know
What glories shine in him,
Pant for his presence, as the roe
Pants for the living stream!

What trifles tease me now!
They swarm like summer flies,
They cleave to everything I do,
And swim before my eyes.

How dull the Sabbath day,
Without the Sabbath's LORD!
How toilsome then to sing and pray,
And wait upon the word!

Of all the truths I hear
How few delight my taste!
I glean a berry here and there,
But mourn the vintage past.

Yet let me (as I ought)
Still hope to be supplied;
No pleasure else is worth a thought,
Nor shall I be denied.

Though I am but a worm,
Unworthy of his care;
The LORD will my desire perform,
And grant me all my prayer.

Hymn 25
John Newton
Rejoice the soul of thy servant.

When my prayers are a burden and task,
No wonder I little receive;
O LORD, make me willing to ask,
Since thou art so ready to give
Although I am bought with thy blood,
And all thy salvation is mine;
At a distance from thee my chief good,
I wander, and languish, and pine.

Of thy goodness of old when I read,
To those who were sinners like me,
Why may I not wrestle and plead,
With them a partaker to be?
Thine arm is not shortened since then,
And those who believe in thy name,
Ever find thou art Yea, and Amen,
Through all generations the same.

While my spirit within me is pressed
With sorrow, temptation, and fear;
Like John I would flee to thy breast,
Jn 13:25
And pour my complaints in thine ear:
How happy and favored was he,
Who could on thy bosom repose!
Might this favor be granted to me,
I'd smile at the rage of my foes.

I have heard of thy wonderful name,
How great and exalted thou art;
But ah! I confess to my shame,
It faintly impresses my heart:
The beams of thy glory display,
As PETER once saw thee appear;
That transported like him I may say,
"It is good for my soul to be here."
Mt 17:4

What a sorrow and weight didst thou feel,
When nailed, for my sake, to the tree!
My heart sure is harder than steel,

Olney Hymns
To feel no more sorrow for thee:
Oh let me with THOMAS descry
The wounds in thy hands and thy side;
And have feelings like his, when I cry,
"My GOD and my Savior has died!"
Jn 20:28

But if thou hast appointed me still
To wrestle, and suffer, and fight;
Oh make me resigned to thy will,
For all thine appointments are right:
This mercy, at least, I entreat,
That knowing how vile I have been,
I with MARY may wait at thy feet,
Lk 7:38
And weep o'er the pardon of sin.

Hymn 26
William Cowper
Self-acquaintance.

Dear Lord accept a sinful heart,
Which of itself complains
And mourns, with much and frequent smart,
The evil it contains.

There fiery seeds of anger lurk,
Which often hurt my frame;
And wait but for the tempter's work,
To fan them to a flame.

Legality holds out a bribe
To purchase life from thee;
And discontent would fain prescribe
How thou shalt deal with me.

While unbelief withstands thy grace;
And puts the mercy by;
Presumption, with a brow of brass,
Says, "Give me, or I die."

How eager are my thoughts to roam
In quest of what they love!
But ah! when duty calls them home,
How heavily they move!

O, cleanse me in a Savior's blood,
Transform me by thy pow'r,
And make me thy beloved abode,
And let me rove no more.

Hymn 27
John Newton
Bitter and sweet.

Kindle, Savior, in my heart
A flame of love divine;
Hear, hear, for mine I trust thou art,
And sure I would be thine:
If my soul has felt thy grace,
If to me thy name is known;
Why should trifles fill the place,
Due to thyself alone.

'Tis a strange mysterious life
I live from day to day;
Light and darkness, peace and strife,
Bear an alternate sway;
When I think the battle won
I have to fight it o'er again;
When I say I'm overthrown,
Relief I soon obtain.

Often at the mercy-seat
While calling on thy name;
Swarms of evil thoughts I meet,
Which fill my soul with shame.
Agitated in my mind,
Like a feather in the air;
Can I thus a blessing find?
My soul, can this be prayer?

But When CHRIST, my LORD and Friend,
Is pleased to show his pow'r;
All at once my troubles end,
And I've a golden hour:
Then I see his smiling face,
Feel the pledge of joys to come;
Often, LORD, repeat this grace
Till thou shalt call me home.

Hymn 28
William Cowper
Prayer for patience.

Lord, who hast suffered all for me,
My peace and pardon to procure;
The lighter cross I bear for thee,
Help me with patience to endure.

The storm of loud repining hush,
I would in humble silence mourn;
Why should th' unburnt, though burning bush,
Be angry as the crackling thorn?

Man should not faint at thy rebuke,
Like Joshua falling on his face,
Josh 7:1-6
When the cursed thing that Achan took,
Brought Israel into just disgrace.

Perhaps some golden wedge suppressed,
Some secret sin offends my GOD;
Perhaps that Babylonish vest,
Self-righteousness, provokes the rod.

Ah! were I buffeted all day,
Mocked, crowned with thorns, and spit upon;
I yet should have no right to say,
My great distress is mine alone.

Let me not angrily declare
No pain was ever sharp like mine;
Nor murmur at the cross I hear,
But rather weep rememb'ring thine.

Hymn 29
William Cowper
Submission.

O Lord, my best desire fulfill
And help me to resign,
Life, health, and comfort to thy will,
And make thy pleasure mine.

Why should I shrink at thy command,
Whose love forbids my fears?
Or tremble at the gracious hand
That wipes away my tears?

No, let me rather freely yield
What most I prize to thee;
Who never hast a good withheld,
Or wilt withhold from me.

Thy favor, all my journey through,
Thou art engaged to grant;
What else I want, or think I do,
'Tis better still to want.

Wisdom and mercy guide my way,
Shall I resist them both?
A poor blind creature of a day,
And crushed before the moth!

But ah! my inward spirit cries,
Still bind me to thy sway;
Else the next cloud that veils my skies,
Drives all these thoughts away.

Hymn 30
John Newton
Why should I complain?

When my Savior, my Shepherd is near,
How quickly my sorrows depart!
New beauties around me appear,
New spirits enliven my heart:
His presence gives peace to my soul,
And Satan assaults me in vain;
While my Shepherd his pow'r controls,
I think I no more shall complain.

But alas! what a change do I find,
When my Shepherd withdraws from my sight?
My fears all return to my mind,
My day is soon changed into night:
Then Satan his efforts renews
To vex and ensnare me again;
All my pleasing enjoyments I lose,
And can only lament and complain.

By these changes I often pass through,
I am taught my own weakness to know;
I am taught what my Shepherd can do,
And how much to his mercy I owe:
It is he who supports me through all,
When I faint he revives me again;
He attends to my prayer when I call,
And bids me no longer complain.

Wherefore then should I murmur and grieve?
Since my Shepherd is always the same,
And has promised he never will leave
Jer 1:19
The soul that confides in his name:
To relieve me from all that I fear,
He was buffeted, tempted, and slain;
And at length he will surely appear,
Though he leaves me awhile to complain.

While I dwell in an enemy's land,
Can I hope to be always in peace?
'Tis enough that my Shepherd's at hand,
And that shortly this warfare will cease;

Olney Hymns
Rev 2:10

For ere long he will bid me remove
From this region of sorrow and pain,
To abide in his presence above,
And then I no more shall complain.

Hymn 31
John Newton
Return, O LORD, how long.

Return to bless my waiting eyes,
And cheer my mourning heart, O LORD!
Without thee, all beneath the skies
No real pleasure can afford.

When thy loved presence meets my sight,
It softens care, and sweetens toil;
The sun shines forth with double light,
The whole creation wears a smile.

Upon thine arm of love I rest,
Thy gracious voice forbids my fear;
No storms disturb my peaceful breast,
No foes assault when thou art near.

But ah! since thou hast been away,
Nothing but trouble have I known;
And Satan marks me for his prey
Because he sees me left alone.

My sun is hid, my comforts lost,
My graces droop, my sins revive;
Distressed, dismayed, and tempest-tossed,
My soul is only just alive!

LORD, hear my cry and come again!
Put all mine enemies to shame,
And let them see, 'tis not in vain
That I have trusted in thy name.

Hymn 32
John Newton
Cast down, but not destroyed.

Though sore beset with guilt and fear,
I cannot, dare not, quite despair;
If I must perish, would the Lord
Have taught my heart to love his word?
Would he have giv'n me eyes to see
Judg 13:23
My danger, and my remedy,
Revealed his name, and bid me pray,
Had he resolved to say me nay?

No--though cast down I am not slain;
I fall, but I shall rise again;
Mic 7:8
The present Satan is thy hour,
But Jesus shall control thy pow'r:
His love will plead for my relief,
He hears my groans, he sees my grief;
Nor will he suffer thee to boast,
A soul, that sought his help, was lost.

'Tis true, I have unfaithful been,
And grieved his Spirit by my sin;
Yet still his mercy he'll reveal,
And all my wounds and follies heal:
Abounding sin, I must confess,
Rom 5:20
But more abounding is his grace;
He once vouchsafed for me to bleed,
And now he lives my cause to plead.

I'll cast myself before his feet,
I see him on his mercy-seat,
('Tis sprinkled with atoning blood)
There sinners find access to God:
Ye burdened souls approach with me,
And make the Savior's name your plea;
JESUS will pardon all who come,
And strike our fierce accuser dumb.

Hymn 33
John Newton
The benighted traveller.

Forest beasts, that live by prey,
Seldom show themselves by day;
But when day-light is withdrawn,
Ps 104:20
Then they rove and roar till dawn.

Who can tell the traveller's fears,
When their horrid yells he hears?
Terror almost stops his breath,
While each step he looks for death.

Thus when Jesus is in view,
Cheerful I my way pursue;
Walking by my Savior's light,
Nothing can my soul affright.

But when he forbears to shine,
Soon the travell'rs case is mine;
Lost, benighted, struck with dread,
What a painful path I tread!

Then, my soul with terror hears
Worse than lions, wolves, or bears,
Roaring loud in every part,
Through the forest of my heart.

Wrath, impatience, envy, pride,
Satan and his host beside,
Press around me to devour;
How can I escape their pow'r?

Gracious LORD afford me light,
Put these beasts of prey to flight;
Let thy pow'r and love be shown,
Save me, for I am thine own.

Hymn 34
John Newton
The prisoner.

When the poor pris'ner through a grate
Sees others walk at large;
How does he mourn his lonely state,
And long for a discharge?

Thus I, confined in unbelief,
My loss of freedom mourn;
And spend my hours in fruitless grief,
Until my Lord return.

The beam of day, which pierces through
The gloom in which I dwell;
Only discloses to my view,
The horrors of my cell.

Ah! how my pensive spirit faints,
To think of former days!
When I could triumph with the saints,
And join their songs of praise!

But now my joys are all cut off,
In prison I am cast;
And Satan, with a cruel scoff,
Ps 140:2
Says, "Where's your God at last?"

Dear Savior, for thy mercies sake,
My strong, my only plea,
These gates and bars in pieces break,
Ps 147:7
And set the pris'ner free!

Surely my soul shall sing to thee,
For liberty restored;
And all thy saints admire to see
The mercies of the LORD.

Hymn 35
John Newton
Perplexity relieved.

Uncertain how the way to find
Which to salvation led;
I listened long, with anxious mind,
To hear what others said.

When some of joys and comforts told
I feared that I was wrong;
For I was stupid, dead, and cold,
Had neither joy nor song.

The Lord my lab'ring heart relieved,
And made my burden light;
Then for a moment I believed,
Supposing all was right.

Of fierce temptations others talked,
Of anguish and dismay;
Through what distresses they had walked,
Before they found the way.

Ah! then I thought my hopes were vain,
For I had lived at ease;
I wished for all my fears again,
To make me more like these.

I had my wish, the LORD disclosed
The evils of my heart;
And left my naked soul, exposed
To Satan's fiery dart.

Alas! "I now must give it up,"
I cried in deep despair;
How could I dream of drawing hope,
From what I cannot bear!

Again my Savior brought me aid,
And when he set me free;
"Trust simply on my word, he said,
And leave the rest to me."

Hymn 36
John Newton
Prayer answered by crosses.

I asked the LORD that I might grow
In faith, and love, and every grace;
Might more of his salvation know,
And seek, more earnestly, his face.

'Twas he who taught me thus to pray,
And he, I trust, has answered prayer!
But it has been in such a way,
As almost drove me to despair.

I hoped that in some favored hour,
At once he'd answer my request;
And by his love's constraining pow'r,
Subdue my sins, and give me rest.

Instead of this, he made me feel
The hidden evils of my heart;
And let the angry pow'rs of hell
Assault my soul in every part.

Yea more, with his own hand he seemed
Intent to aggravate my woe;
Crossed all the fair designs I schemed,
Blasted my gourds, and laid me low.

LORD, why is this, I trembling cried,
Wilt thou pursue thy worm to death?
"'Tis in this way, the LORD replied,
I answer prayer for grace and faith.

These inward trials I employ,
From self, and pride, to set thee free;
And break thy schemes of earthly joy,
That thou may'st find thy all in me."

Hymn 37
John Newton
I will trust and not be afraid.

Begone unbelief,
My Savior is near,
And for my relief
Will surely appear:
By prayer let me wrestle,
And he wilt perform,
With CHRIST in the vessel,
I smile at the storm.

Though dark be my way,
Since he is my guide,
'Tis mine to obey,
'Tis his to provide;
Though cisterns be broken,
And creatures all fail,
The word he has spoken
Shall surely prevail.

His love in time past
Forbids me to think
He'll leave me at last
In trouble to sink;
Each sweet Ebenezer
I have in review,
Confirms his good pleasure
To help me quite through.

Determined to save,
He watched o'er my path,
When Satan's blind slave,
I sported with death;
And can he have taught me
To trust in his name,
And thus far have brought me,
To put me to shame?

Why should I complain
Of want or distress,
Temptation or pain?
He told me no less:
The heirs of salvation,

Olney Hymns
I know from his word,
Through much tribulation
Must follow their LORD.
Acts 14:22

How bitter that cup,
No heart can conceive,
Which he drank quite up,
That sinners might live!
His way was much rougher,
And darker than mine;
Did Jesus thus suffer,
And shall I repine?

Since all that I meet
Shall work for my good,
The bitter is sweet,
The med'cine is food;
Though painful at present,
Wilt cease before long,
And then, O! how pleasant,
The conqueror's song!
Rom 8:37

Hymn 38
John Newton
Questions to unbelief.

If to Jesus for relief
My soul has fled by prayer;
Why should I give way to grief,
Or heart-consuming care?
Are not all things in his hand?
Has he not his promise past?
Will he then regardless stand
And let me sink at last?

While I know his providence
Disposes each event;
Shall I judge by feeble sense,
And yield to discontent?
If he worms and sparrows feed,
Clothe the grass in rich array;
Mt 6:26-30
Can he see a child in need,
And turn his eye away?

When his name was quite unknown,
And sin my life employed;
Then he watched me as his own,
Or I had been destroyed:
Now his mercy-seat I know,
Now by grace am reconciled;
Would he spare me while a foe,
Rom 5:10
To leave me when a child?

If he all my wants supplied
When I disdained to pray;
Now his Spirit is my guide,
How can he say me nay?
If he would not give me up,
When my soul against him fought;
Will he disappoint the hope,
Which he himself has wrought?

If he shed his precious blood
To bring me to his fold;
Can I think that meaner good

Olney Hymns
Rom 8:32
He ever will withhold?
Satan, vain is thy device!
Here my hope rests well-assured,
In that great redemption-price,
I see the whole secured.

Hymn 39
John Newton
Great effects by weak means.

Unbelief the soul dismays,
What objections will it raise!
But true faith securely leans
On the promise, in the means.

If to faith it once be known,
God has said, "It shall be done,
And in this appointed way;"
Faith has then no more to say.

Moses' rod, by faith upreared,
Ex 14:21
Through the sea a path prepared;
Jericho's devoted wall,
Josh 6:20
At the trumpet's sound must fall.

With a pitcher and a lamp,
Judg 7:22
Gideon overthrew a camp
And a stone, well aimed by faith,
1Sam 17:29
Proved the armed Philistine's death.

Thus the LORD is pleased to try
Those who on his help rely;
By the means he makes it known,
That the pow'r is all his own.

Yet the means are not in vain,
If the end we would attain;
Though the breath of prayer be weak,
None shall find, but they who seek.

God alone the heart can reach;
Yet the ministers must preach;
'Tis their part the seed to sow,
And 'tis his to make it grow.

Hymn 40
John Newton
Why art thou cast down?

Be still my heart! these anxious cares
To thee are burdens, thorns, and snares,
They cast dishonor on thy Lord,
And contradict his gracious word!

Brought safely by his hand thus far,
Why wilt thou now give place to fear?
How canst thou want if he provide,
Or lose thy way with such a guide?

When first before his mercy-seat,
Thou didst to him thy all commit;
He gave thee warrant, from that hour,
To trust his wisdom, love, and pow'r.

Did ever trouble yet befall,
And he refuse to hear thy call?
And has he not his promise past,
That thou shalt overcome at last?

Like David, thou may'st comfort draw,
Saved from the bear's and lion's paw;
Goliath's rage I may defy,
For God, my Savior, still is nigh.

He who has helped me hitherto,
Will help me all my journey through;
And give me daily cause to raise
New Ebenezers to his praise.

Though rough and thorny be the road,
It leads thee home, apace, to GOD;
Then count thy present trials small,
For heav'n will make amends for all.

Hymn 41
John Newton
The way of access.

One glance of thine, eternal LORD,
Pierces all nature through;
Nor heav'n, nor earth, nor hell, afford
A shelter from thy view!

The mighty whole, each smaller part,
At once before thee lies;
And every thought, of every heart,
Is open to thine eyes.

Though greatly from myself concealed,
Thou see'st my inward frame;
To thee I always stand revealed,
Exactly as I am.

Since therefore I can hardly bear
What in myself I see;
How vile and black must I appear,
Most holy GOD, to thee.

But since my Savior stands between,
In garments dyed in blood;
'Tis he, instead of me, is seen,
When I approach to God.

Thus, though a sinner, I am safe;
He pleads before the throne,
His life and death, in my behalf,
And calls my sins his own.

What wondrous love, what mysteries,
In this appointment shine!
My breaches of the Law are his
2Cor 5:21
And his obedience mine.

Hymn 42
John Newton
The Pilgrim' song.

From Egypt lately freed
By the Redeemer's grace;
A rough and thorny path we tread,
In hopes to see his face.

The flesh dislikes the way,
But faith approves it well;
This only leads to endless day,
All others lead to hell.

The promised land of peace
Faith keeps in constant view;
How different from the wilderness
We now are passing through!

Here often from our eyes
Clouds hide the light divine;
There we shall have unclouded skies,
Our Sun will always shine.

Here griefs, and cares, and pains,
And fears, distress us sore;
But there eternal pleasure reigns,
And we shall weep no more.

LORD pardon our complaints,
We follow at thy call;
The joy, prepared for suff'ring saints,
Will make amends for all.

IV. COMFORT

Hymn 43
John Newton
Faith a new and comprehensive sense.

Sight, hearing, feeling, taste and smell,
Are gifts we highly prize;
But faith does singly each excel,
And all the five comprise.

More piercing than the eagle's flight
It views the world unknown;
Surveys the glorious realms of light,
And Jesus on the throne.

It hears the mighty voice of God,
And ponders what he saith
His word and works, his gifts and rod,
Have each a voice to faith.

It feels the touch of heavenly pow'r,
Lk 8:46
And from that boundless source,
Derives fresh vigor every hour,
To run its daily course.

The truth and goodness of the Lord,
Are suited to its taste
Ps 119:103
Mean is the worldling's pampered board,
To faith's perpetual feast.

It smells the dear Redeemer's name
Like ointment poured forth;
SS 1:3
Faith only knows or can proclaim,
Its favor or its worth.

Till saving faith possess the mind,
In vain of sense we boast;
We are but senseless, tasteless, blind,
And deaf, and dead, and lost.

Hymn 44
William Cowper
The happy change.

How blest thy creature is, O God,
When with a single eye,
He views the lustre of thy word,
The day-spring from on high!

Through all the storms that veil the skies,
And frown on earthly things;
The Sun of righteousness he eyes,
With healing on his wings.

Struck by that light, the human heart,
Isa 35:7
A barren soil no more;
Sends the sweet smell of grace abroad,
Where serpents lurked before.

The soul, a dreary province once
Of Satan's dark domain;
Feels a new empire formed within,
And owns a heav'nly reign.

The glorious orb, whose golden beams,
The fruitful year control
Since first obedient to thy word,
He started from the goal;

Has cheered the nations, with the joys
His orient rays impart
But Jesus, 'tis thy light alone,
Can shine upon the heart.

Hymn 45
William Cowper
Retirement.

Far from the world, O Lord, I flee,
From strife and tumult far;
From scenes, where Satan wages still,
His most successful war.

The calm retreat, the silent shade,
With prayer and praise agree;
And seem, by thy sweet bounty made,
For those who follow thee.

There if thy Spirit touch the soul,
And grace her mean abode;
Oh with what peace, and joy, and love,
She communes with her God!

There like the nightingale she pours
Her solitary lays,
Nor asks a witness of her song,
Nor thirsts for human praise.

Author and Guardian of my life,
Sweet source of light divine;
And (all harmonious names in one)
My Savior, thou art mine!

What thanks I owe thee, and what love,
A boundless, endless store;
Shall echo through the realms above,
When time shall be no more.

Hymn 46
John Newton
JESUS my all.

Why should I fear the darkest hour,
Or tremble at the tempter's pow'r?
Jesus vouchsafes to be my tow'r.

Though hot the fight; why quit the field?
Why must I either flee or yield,
Since JESUS is my mighty shield?

When creature comforts fade and die,
Worldlings may weep; but why should I?
Jesus still lives, and still is nigh.

Though all the flocks and herds were dead,
My soul a famine need not dread,
For Jesus is my living bread.

I know not what may soon betide,
Or how my wants shall be supplied;
But Jesus knows, and will provide.

Though sin would fill me with distress,
The throne of grace I dare address;
For JESUS is my righteousness.

Though faint my prayers, and cold my love,
My stedfast hope shall not remove,
While Jesus intercedes above.

Against me earth and hell combine,
But on my side is pow'r divine;
Jesus is all, and he is mine.

Hymn 47
William Cowper
The hidden life.

To tell the Savior all my wants,
How pleasing is the task?
Nor less to praise him when he grants
Beyond what I can ask.

My lab'ring spirit vainly seeks
To tell but half the joy;
With how much tenderness he speaks,
And helps me to reply.

Nor were it wise, nor should I choose
Such secrets to declare;
Like precious wines their taste they lose
Exposed to open air.

But this with boldness I proclaim,
Nor care if thousands hear;
Sweet is the ointment of his name,
Not life is half so dear.

And can you frown, my former friends,
Who knew what once I was;
And blame the song that thus commends
The man who bore the cross.

Trust me, I draw the likeness true,
And not as fancy paints,
Such honor may he give to you,
For such have all his saints.

Hymn 48
William Cowper
Joy and peace in believing.

Sometimes a light surprises
The christian while he sings;
It is the LORD who rises
With healing in his wings:
When comforts are declining,
He grants the soul again
A season of clear shining
To cheer it after rain.

In holy contemplation,
We sweetly then pursue
The theme of God's salvation,
And find it ever new:
Set free from present sorrow,
We cheerfully can say,
E'en let th' unknown tomorrow,
Mt 6:34
Bring with it what it may.

It can bring with it nothing
But he will bear us through;
Who gives the lilies clothing
Will clothe his people too:
Beneath the spreading heavens,
No creature but is fed;
And he who feeds the ravens,
Will give his children bread.

The vine, nor fig-tree neither,
Hab 3:17,18
Their wonted fruit should bear,
Though all the fields should wither,
Nor flocks, nor herds, be there:
Yet God the same abiding,
His praise shall tune my voice;
For while in him confiding,
I cannot but rejoice.

Hymn 49
William Cowper
True pleasures.

Lord my soul with pleasure springs,
When Jesus' name I hear;
And when God the Spirit brings
The word of promise near.
Beauties too, in holiness,
Still delighted I perceive;
Nor have words that can express
The joys thy precepts give.

Clothed in sanctity and grace,
How sweet it is to see
Those who love thee as they pass,
Or when they wait on thee:
Pleasant too, to sit and tell
What we owe to love divine;
Till our grateful bosoms swell,
And eyes begin to shine.

Those the comforts I possess,
Which God shall still increase;
All his ways are pleasantness,
Pr 3:17
And all his paths are peace:
Nothing JESUS did or spoke,
Henceforth let me ever slight;
For I love his easy yoke,
Mt 11:30
And find his burden light.

Hymn 50
William Cowper
The Christian.

Honor and happiness unite
To make the christian's name a praise;
How fair the scene, how clear the light,
That fills the remnant of his days!

A kingly character he bears,
No change his priestly office knows;
Unfading is the crown he wears,
His joys can never reach a close.

Adorned with glory from on high,
Salvation shines upon his face;
His robe is of th' ethereal dye,
His steps are dignity and grace.

Inferior honors he disdains,
Nor stoops to take applause from earth,
The King of kings himself, maintains
Th' expenses of his heav'nly birth.

The noblest creature seen below,
Ordained to fill a throne above;
GOD gives him all he can bestow,
His kingdom of eternal love!

My soul is ravished at the thought!
Methinks from earth I see him rise;
Angels congratulate his lot,
And shout him welcome to the skies!

Hymn 51

William Cowper
Lively hope, and gracious fear.

I was a groveling creature once,
And safely cleaved to earth;
I wanted spirit to renounce
The clod that gave me birth.

But God has breathed upon a worm,
And sent me, from above,
Wings, such as clothe an angel's form,
The wings of joy and love.

With these to Pisgah's top I fly,
And there delighted stand;
To view, beneath a shining sky,
The spacious promised land.

The LORD of all the vast domain,
Has promised it to me;
The length and breadth of all the plain,
As far as faith can see.

How glorious is my privilege!
To thee for help I call,
I stand upon a mountain's edge,
O save me, lest I fall!

Though much exalted in the LORD,
My strength is not my own;
Then let me tremble at his word,
And none shall cast me down.

Hymn 52
John Newton
Confidence.

Yes! since God himself has said it,
On the promise I rely;
His good word demands my credit,
What can unbelief reply?
He is strong and can fulfill,
He is truth and therefore will.

As to all the doubts and questions,
Which my spirit often grieve,
These are Satan's sly suggestions,
And I need no answer give;
He would fain destroy my hope,
But the promise bears it up.

Sure the LORD thus far has brought me
By his watchful tender care;
Sure 'tis he himself has taught me
How to seek his face by prayer:
After so much mercy past,
Will he give me up at last?

True, I've been a foolish creature;
And have sinned against his grace;
But forgiveness is his nature,
Though he justly hides his face:
Ere he called me well he knew,
Isa 48:8
What a heart like mine would do.

In my Savior's intercession
Therefore I will still confide;
LORD accept my free contrition,
I have sinned, but thou hast died:
Rom 8:34
This is all I have to plead,
This is all the plea I need.

Hymn 53
John Newton
Peace restored.

O, speak that gracious word again,
And cheer my drooping heart!
No voice but thine can soothe my pain,
Or bid my fears depart.

And canst thou still vouchsafe to own
A wretch so vile as I?
And may I still approach thy throne,
And Abba, Father, cry?

Oh then let saints and angels join,
And help me to proclaim,
The grace that healed a breach like mine,
And put my foes to shame!

How oft did Satan's cruel boast
My troubled soul affright!
He told me I was surely lost,
And GOD had left me quite.
Ps 71:11

Guilt made me fear, lest all were true
The lying tempter said!
But now the LORD appears in view,
My enemy is fled.

My Savior, by his pow'rful word,
Has turned my night to day;
And his salvation's joys restored,
Which I had sinned away.

Dear LORD I wonder and adore,
Thy grace is all divine;
Oh keep me, that I sin no more
Against such love as thine!

Hymn 54

John Newton
Hear what he has done for my soul!

Saved by blood I live to tell,
What the love of CHRIST hath done;
He redeemed my soul from hell,
Of a rebel made a son:
O, I tremble still, to think
How secure I lived in sin;
Sporting on destruction's brink,
Yet preserved from falling in.

In his own appointed hour,
To my heart the Savior spoke,
Touched me by his Spirit's pow'r,
And my dang'rous slumber broke.
Then I saw and owned my guilt,
Soon my gracious LORD replied;
"Fear not, I my blood have spilt,
'Twas for such as thee I died."

Shame and wonder, joy and love,
All at once possessed my heart;
Can I hope thy grace to prove,
After acting such a part?
"Thou hast greatly sinned, he said,
But I freely all forgive;
I myself thy debt have paid,
Now I bid thee rise and live."

Come, my fellow-sinners, try,
JESUS' heart is full of love;
Oh that you, as well as I,
May his wondrous mercy prove!
He has sent me to declare,
All is ready, all is free;
Why should any soul despair,
When he saved a wretch like me?

Hymn 55

John Newton
Freedom from care.

While I lived without the Lord,
(If I might be said to live)
Nothing could relief afford,
Nothing satisfaction give.

Empty hopes and groundless fear,
Moved by turns my anxious mind;
Like a feather in the air,
Made the sport of every wind.

Now, I see, whate'er betide,
All is well if CHRIST be mine;
He has promised to provide,
I have only to resign.

When a sense of sin and thrall,
Forced me to the sinner's Friend;
He engaged to manage all,
By the way, and to the end.

"Cast, he said, on me thy care,
Ps 55:22
'Tis enough that I am nigh;
I will all thy burdens bear,
I will all thy wants supply.

Simply follow as I lead,
Do not reason but believe;
Call on me in time of need,
Thou shalt surely help receive."

Lord I would, I do, submit,
Gladly yield my all to thee;
What thy wisdom sees most fit,
Must be, surely, best for me.

Only when the way is rough,
And the coward flesh would start,
Let thy promise and thy love,
Cheer and animate my heart.

Hymn 56
John Newton
Humiliation and praise.
(Imitated from the German.)

When the wounded spirit hears
The voice of JESUS' blood;
How the message stops the tears
Which else in vain had flowed:
Pardon, grace, and peace proclaimed,
And the sinner called a child;
Then the stubborn heart is tamed,
Renewed, and reconciled.

O! 'twas grace indeed, to spare,
And save a wretch like me!
Men or angels could not bear
What I have offered thee:
Were thy bolts at their command,
Hell, ere now, had been my place;
Thou alone couldst silent stand,
And wait to show thy grace.

If in one created mind
The tenderness and love
Of thy saints on earth were joined,
With all the hosts above;
Still that love were weak and poor,
If compared, my LORD, with thine;
Far too scanty to endure
A heart so vile as mine.

Wondrous mercy I have found,
But ah! how faint my praise!
Must I be a cumber-ground,
Unfruitful all my days?
Do I in thy garden grow,
Yet produce thee only leaves?
LORD, forbid it should he so!
The thought my spirit grieves.

Heavy charges Satan brings
To fill me with distress;
Let me hide beneath thy wings,
And plead thy righteousness:

John Newton

LORD, to thee for help I call,
'Tis thy promise bids me come;
Tell him thou hast paid for all,
And that shall strike him dumb.

Hymn 57
William Cowper
For the poor.

When Hagar found the bottle spent,
Gen 21:19
And wept o'er Ishmael;
A message from the Lord was sent
To guide her to a well.

Should not Elijah's cake and cruse,
1Ki 17:14
Convince us at this day,
A gracious God will not refuse,
Provisions by the way?

His saints and servants shall be fed,
The promise is secure;
"Bread shall be given them, he has said,
Their water shall be sure."
Isa 33:16

Repasts far richer they shall prove
Than all earth's dainties are;
'Tis sweet to taste a Savior's love,
Though in the meanest fare.

To JESUS then your trouble bring,
Nor murmur at your lot;
While you art poor, and he is King,
You shall not be forgot.

Hymn 58
John Newton
Home in view.

As when the weary travell'r gains
The height of some o'er-looking hill;
His heart revives, if cross the plains
He eyes his home, though distant still.

While he surveys the much-loved spot,
He slights the space that lies between;
His past fatigues are now forgot,
Because his journey's end is seen.

Thus, when the christian pilgrim views
By faith, his mansion in the skies;
The sight his fainting strength renews,
And wings his speed to reach the prize.

The thought of home his spirit cheers,
No more he grieves for troubles past;
Nor any future trial fears,
Acts 20:24
So he may safe arrive at last.

'Tis there, he says, I am to dwell
With JESUS, in the realms of day;
Then I shall bid my cares farewell,
And he will wipe my tears away.

Jesus, on thee our hope depends,
To lead us on to thine abode;
Assured our home will make amends
For all our toil while on the road.

V. DEDICATION and SURRENDER

Hymn 59
John Newton
Old things are passed away.

Let worldly minds the world pursue,
It has no charms for me;
Once I admired its trifles too,
But grace has set me free.

Its pleasures now no longer please,
No more content afford;
Far from my heart be joys like these;
Now I have seen the LORD.

As by the light of op'ning day
The stars are all concealed;
So earthly pleasures fade away,
When JESUS is revealed.

Creatures no more divide my choice,
I bid them all depart;
His name, and love, and gracious voice,
Have fixed my roving heart.

Now, Lord, I would be thine alone,
And wholly live to thee;
But may I hope that thou wilt own
A worthless worm, like me?

Yes! though of sinners I'm the worst,
I cannot doubt thy will;
For if thou hadst not loved me first
I had refused thee still.
Jer 31:3

Hymn 60
John Newton
The power of grace.

Happy the birth where grace presides
To form the future life!
In wisdom's paths the soul she guides,
Remote from noise and strife.

Since I have known the Savior's name
And what for me he bore;
No more I toil for empty fame,
I thirst for gold no more.

Placed by his hand in this retreat,
I make his love my theme;
And see that all the world calls great,
Is but a waking dream.

Since be has ranked my worthless name
Amongst his favored few;
Let the mad world who scoff at them
Revile and hate me too.

O thou whose voice the dead can raise,
And soften hearts of stone,
And teach the dumb to sing thy praise,
This work is all thine own!

Thy wond'ring saints rejoice to see
A wretch, like me, restored
And point, and say, "How changed is he,
Who once defied the LORD!"

Grace bid me live, and taught my tongue
To aim at notes divine;
And grace accepts my feeble song,
The glory, LORD, be thine!

Hymn 61
William Cowper
My soul thirsteth for God.

I thirst, but not as once I did,
The vain delights of earth to share;
Thy wounds, EMMANUEL, all forbid,
That I should seek my pleasures there.

It was the sight of thy dear cross,
First weaned my soul from earthly things;
And taught me to esteem as dross,
The mirth of fools and pomp of kings.

I want that grace that springs from thee,
That quickens all things where it flows;
And makes a wretched thorn, like me,
Bloom as the myrtle, or the rose.

Dear fountain of delight unknown!
No longer sink below the brim;
But overflow, and pour me down
A living, and life-giving stream!

For sure, of all the plants that share
The notice of thy Father's eye;
None proves less grateful to his care,
Or yields him meaner fruit than I.

Hymn 62
William Cowper
Love constraining to obedience.

No strength of nature can suffice
To serve the LORD aright;
And what she has, she misapplies,
For want of clearer light.

How long beneath the law I lay
In bondage and distress!
I toiled the precept to obey,
But toiled without success.

Then to abstain from outward sin
Was more than I could do;
Now, if I feel its pow'r within,
I feel I hate it too.

Then all my servile works were done
A righteousness to raise;
Now, freely chosen in the Son,
I freely choose his ways.

What shall I do was then the word,
That I may worthier grow?
What shall I render to the LORD?
Is my enquiry now.

To see the Law by CHRIST fulfilled,
And hear his pard'ning voice;
Changes a slave into a child,
Rom 3:31
And duty into choice.

Hymn 63
William Cowper
The heart healed and changed by mercy.

Sin enslaved me many years,
And led me bound and blind;
Till at length a thousand fears
Came swarming o'er my mind.
Where, I said in deep distress,
Will these sinful pleasures end?
How shall I secure my peace,
And make the LORD my friend?

Friends and ministers said much
The gospel to enforce;
But my blindness still was such,
I chose a legal course
Much I fasted, watched and strove,
Scarce would show my face abroad,
Feared, almost, to speak or move,
A stranger still to GOD.

Thus afraid to trust his grace,
Long time did I rebel;
Till, despairing of my case,
Down at his feet I fell:
Then my stubborn heart he broke,
And subdued me to his sway;
By a simple word he spoke,
"Thy sins are done away."

Hymn 64
William Cowper
Hatred of sin.

Holy LORD GOD! I love thy truth,
Nor dare thy least commandment slight;
Yet pierced by sin, the serpent's tooth,
I mourn the anguish of the bite.

But though the poison lurks within,
Hope bids me still with patience wait;
Till death shall set me free from sin,
Free from the only thing I hate.

Had I a throne above the rest,
Where angels and archangels dwell;
One sin, unslain, within my breast,
Would make that heav'n as dark as hell.

The pris'ner, sent to breathe fresh air,
And blessed with liberty again,
Would mourn, were he condemned to wear
One link of all his former chain.

But O! no foe invades the bliss,
When glory crowns the christian's head;
One view of Jesus as he is,
Will strike all sin for ever dead.

Hymn 65
John Newton
The child
Ps 131:2 Mt 18:3,4

Quiet, LORD, my froward heart,
Make me teachable and mild,
Upright, simple, free from art,
Make me as a weaned child:
From distrust and envy free,
Pleased with all that pleases thee.

What thou shalt today provide,
Let me as a child receive;
What tomorrow may betide,
Calmly to thy wisdom leave:
'Tis enough that thou wilt care,
Why should I the burden bear?

As a little child relies
On a care beyond his own;
Knows he's neither strong nor wise,
Fears to stir a step alone:
Let me thus with thee abide,
As my Father, Guard, and Guide.

Thus preserved from Satan's wiles,
Safe from dangers, free from fears;
May I live upon thy smiles,
Till the promised hour appears;
When the sons of God shall prove
All their Father's boundless love.

Hymn 66
John Newton
True happiness.

Fix my heart and eyes on thine!
What are other objects worth?
But to see thy glory shine,
Is a heav'n begun on earth:
Trifles can no longer move,
O, I tread on all beside,
When I feel my Saviour's love,
And remember how he died.

Now my search is at an end,
Now my wishes rove no more!
Thus my moments I would spend,
Love, and wonder, and adore:
Jesus, source of excellence!
All thy glorious love reveal!
Kingdoms shall not bribe me hence,
While this happiness I feel.

Take my heart, 'tis all thine own,
To thy will my spirit frame;
Thou shalt reign, and thou alone,
Over all I have, or am:
If a foolish thought shall dare
To rebel against thy word,
Slay it, LORD; and do not spare,
Let it feel thy Spirit's sword.

Making thus the LORD my choice,
I have nothing more to choose,
But to listen to thy voice,
And my will in thine to lose:
Thus, whatever may betide,
I shall safe and happy be;
Still content and satisfied,
Having all, in having thee.

Hymn 67
John Newton
The happy debtor.

Ten thousand talents once I owed,
And nothing had to pay;
But JESUS freed me from the load,
And washed my debt away.

Yet since the LORD forgave my sin,
And blotted out my score;
Much more indebted I have been,
Than e'er I was before.

My guilt is cancelled quite, I know,
And satisfaction made;
But the vast debt of love I owe,
Can never be repaid.

The love I owe for sin forgiv'n,
For power to believe,
For present peace, and promised heav'n,
No angel can conceive.

That love of thine! thou sinner's Friend!
Witness thy bleeding heart!
My little all can ne'er extend
To pay a thousandth part.

Nay more, the poor returns I make
I first from thee obtain;
1Chr 29:14
And 'tis of grace, that thou wilt take
Such poor returns again.

'Tis well--it shall my glory be
(Let who will boast their store)
In time and to eternity,
To owe thee more and more.

VI. CAUTIONS

Hymn 68
William Cowper
The new convert.

The new-born child of gospel-grace,
Like some fair tree when summer's nigh,
Beneath EMMANUEL's shining face,
Lifts up his blooming branch on high.

No fears he feels, he sees no foes,
No conflict yet his faith employs,
Nor has he learnt to whom he owes,
The strength and peace his soul enjoys.

But sin soon darts its cruel sting,
And comforts sinking day by day;
What seemed his own, a self-fed spring,
Proves but a brook that glides away.

When Gideon armed his num'rous host,
The LORD soon made his numbers less;
And said, lest Israel vainly boast,
Judg 7:2
"My arm procured me this success."

Thus will he bring our spirits down,
And draw our ebbing comforts low;
That saved by grace, but not our own,
We may not claim the praise we owe.

Hymn 69
William Cowper
True and false comforts.

O God, whose favorable eye
The sin-sick soul revives;
Holy and heav'nly is the joy
Thy shining presence gives.

Not such as hypocrites suppose,
Who with a graceless heart,
Taste not of thee, but drink a dose
Prepared by Satan's art.

Intoxicating joys are theirs,
Who while they boast their light,
And seem to soar above the stars,
Are plunging into night.

Lulled in a soft and fatal sleep,
They sin, and yet rejoice;
Were they indeed the Savior's sheep,
Would they not hear his voice?

Be mine the comforts, that reclaim
The soul from Satan's pow'r;
That make me blush for what I am,
And hate my sin the more.

'Tis joy enough, my All in All,
At thy dear feet to lie;
Thou wilt not let me lower fall,
And none can higher fly.

Hymn 70
John Newton
True and false zeal.

Zeal is that pure and heav'nly flame,
The fire of love supplies;
While that which often bears the name,
Is self in a disguise.

True zeal is merciful and mild,
Can pity and forbear;
The false is headstrong, fierce and wild,
And breathes revenge and war.

While zeal for truth the christian warms,
He knows the worth of peace;
But self contends for names and forms,
Its party to increase.

Zeal has attained its highest aim,
Its end is satisfied;
If sinners love the Savior's name,
Nor seeks it ought betide.

But self, however well employed,
Has its own ends in view;
And says, as boasting Jehu cried,
2Ki 10:16
"Come, see what I can do."

Self may its poor reward obtain,
And be applauded here;
But zeal the best applause will gain,
When JESUS shall appear.

Dear LORD, the idol self dethrone,
And from our hearts remove;
And let no zeal by us be shown,
But that which springs from love.

Hymn 71
William Cowper
A living and a dead faith.

The LORD receives his highest praise,
From humble minds and hearts sincere;
While all the loud professor says,
Offends the righteous Judge's ear.

To walk as children of the day
To mark the precepts' holy light
To wage the warfare, watch and pray,
Show who are pleasing in his sight.

Not words alone it cost the LORD,
To purchase pardon for his own;
Nor with a soul, by grace restored,
Return the Savior words alone.

With golden bells, the priestly vest,
Ex 28:33
And rich pomegranates bordered round,
The need of holiness expressed,
And called for fruit, as well as sound.

Easy, indeed, it were to reach
A mansion in the courts above,
If swelling words, and fluent speech
Might serve, instead of faith and love.

But none shall gain the blissful place,
Or GOD'S unclouded glory see;
Who talks of free and sovereign grace,
Unless that grace has made him free.

Hymn 72
William Cowper
Abuse of the gospel.

Too many, LORD, abuse thy grace,
In this licentious day;
And while they boast they see thy face,
They turn their own away.

Thy Book displays a gracious light
That can the blind restore;
But these are dazzled by the sight,
And blinded still the more.

The pardon, such presume upon,
They do not beg, but steal;
And when they plead it at thy throne,
O, where's the Spirit's seal?

Was it for this, ye lawless tribe,
The dear Redeemer bled;
Is this the grace the saints imbibe
From CHRIST the living head?

Ah Lord, we know thy chosen few
Are fed with heav'nly fare;
But these, the wretched husks they chew,
Proclaim them what they are.

The liberty our hearts implore
Is not to live in sin;
But still to wait at wisdom's door,
Till mercy calls us in.

Hymn 73
William Cowper
The narrow way.

What thousands never knew the road!
What thousands hate it when 'tis known!
None but the chosen tribes of God,
Will seek or choose it for their own.

A thousand ways in ruin end,
One, only, leads to joys on high;
By that my willing steps ascend,
Pleased with a journey to the sky.

No more I ask, or hope to find,
Delight or happiness below;
Sorrow may well possess the mind
That feeds where thorns and thistles grow.

The joy that fades is not for me,
I seek immortal joys above;
There, glory without end, shall be
The bright reward of faith and love.

Cleave to the world ye sordid worms,
Contented lick your native dust;
But God shall fight, with all his storms,
Against the idol of your trust.

Hymn 74
William Cowper
Dependance.

To keep the lamp alive
With oil we fill the bowl;
'Tis water makes the willow thrive,
And grace that feeds the soul.

The LORD'S unsparing hand
Supplies the living stream
It is not at our own command,
But still derived from him.

Beware of Peter's word,
Mt 26:33
Nor confidently say,
"I never will deny thee, LORD,"
But grant I never may.

Man's wisdom is to seek
His strength in God alone;
And e'en an angel would be weak,
Who trusted in his own.

Retreat beneath his wings,
And in his grace confide;
This more exalts the King of kings
Jn 6:29
Than all your works beside.

In JESUS is our store,
Grace issues from his throne;
Whoever says, "I want no more,"
Confesses he has none.

Hymn 75
William Cowper
Not of works.

Grace, triumphant in the throne,
Scorns a rival, reigns alone!
Come and bow beneath her sway,
Cast your idol works away:
Works of man, when made his plea,
Never shall accepted be;
Fruits of pride (vain-glorious worm)
Are the best he can perform.

Self, the god his soul adores,
Influences all his pow'rs;
JESUS is a slighted name,
Self-advancement all his aim:
But when God the Judge shall come,
To pronounce the final doom
Then for rocks and hills to hide,
All his works and all his pride.

Still the boasting heart replies,
What the worthy and the wise,
Friends to temperance and peace,
Have not these a righteousness?
Banish every vain pretence
Built on human excellence;
Perish everything in man,
But the grace that never can.

Hymn 76
John Newton
Sin's deceit.

Sin, when viewed by scripture light,
Is a horrid, hateful sight;
But when seen in Satan's glass,
Then it wears a pleasing face.

When the gospel trumpet sounds,
When I think how grace abounds,
When I feel sweet peace within,
Then I'd rather die than sin.

When the cross I view by faith,
Sin is madness, poison, death;
Tempt me not, 'tis all in vain,
Sure I ne'er can yield again.

Satan, for awhile debarred,
When he finds me off my guard,
Puts his glass before my eyes,
Quickly other thoughts arise.

What before excited fears,
Rather pleasing now appears;
If a sin, it seems so small,
Or, perhaps, no sin at all.

Often thus, through sin's deceit,
Grief, and shame, and loss I meet,
Like a fish, my soul mistook,
Saw the bait, but not the hook.

O my LORD, what shall I say?
How can I presume to pray?
Not a word have I to plead,
Sins, like mine, are black indeed!

Made, by past experience, wise,
Let me learn thy word to prize;
Taught by what I've felt before,
Let me Satan's glass abhor.

Hymn 77
John Newton
Are there few that shall he saved?

Destruction's dangerous road
What multitudes pursue!
While that which leads the soul to God,
Is known or sought by few.

Believers enter in
By CHRIST, the living gate;
But they who will not leave their sin,
Complain it is too strait.

If self must be denied,
And sin forsaken quite;
They rather choose the way that's wide,
And strive to think it right.

Encompassed by a throng,
On numbers they depend;
So many surely can't be wrong,
And miss a happy end.

But numbers are no mark
That men will right be found
A few were saved in Noah's ark,
1Pet 3:20
For many millions drowned.

Obey the gospel call,
And enter while you may;
The flock of CHRIST is always small,
Lk 12:32
And none are safe but they.

LORD, open sinners' eyes
Their awful state to see
And make them, ere the storm arise,
To thee for safety flee.

Hymn 78
John Newton
The sluggard.

The wishes that the sluggard frames,
Prov 6:10; 24:30; 22:13; 20:4
Of course must fruitless prove;
With folded arms he stands and dreams,
But has no heart to move.

His field from others may be known,
The fence is broken through;
The ground with weeds is overgrown,
And no good crop in view.

No hardship, he, or toil, can bear,
No difficulty meet;
He wastes his hours at home, for fear
Of lions in the street.

What wonder then if sloth and sleep,
Distress and famine bring!
Can he in harvest hope to reap,
Who will not sow in spring?

'Tis often thus, in soul concerns,
We gospel-sluggards see;
Who if a wish would serve their turns,
Might true believers be.

But when the preacher bids them watch,
And seek, and strive, and pray,
1Cor 9:24 Lk 13:24
At every poor excuse they catch,
A lion's in the way!

To use the means of grace, how loath!
We call them still in vain;
They yield to their beloved sloth,
And fold their arms again.

Dear Savior, let thy pow'r appear,
The outward call to aid;
These drowsy souls, can only hear
The voice, that wakes the dead.

Hymn 79
John Newton
Not in word, but in power.

How soon the Savior's gracious call,
Disarmed the rage of bloody Saul!
Acts 9:6
JESUS, the knowledge of thy name,
Changes the lion to a lamb!

Zaccheus, when he knew the LORD,
Lk 19:8
What he had gained by wrong, restored;
And of the wealth he prized before,
He gave the half to feed the poor.

The woman who so vile had been,
Lk 7:47
When brought to weep o'er pardoned sin,
Was from her evil ways estranged,
And showed that grace her heart had changed.

And can we think the pow'r of grace
Is lost, by change of time and place?
Then it was mighty, all allow,
And is it but a notion now?

Can they whom pride and passion sway,
Who Mammon and the world obey,
In envy or contention live,
Presume that they indeed believe?

True faith unites to CHRIST the root,
By him producing holy fruit;
And they who no such fruit can show,
Still on the stock of nature grow.

LORD, let thy word effectual prove,
To work in us obedient love!
And may each one who hears it dread
A name to live; and yet be dead.
Rev 3:1

VII. PRAISE

Hymn 80
William Cowper
Praise for faith.

Of all the gifts thine hand bestows,
Thou Giver of all good!
Not heav'n itself a richer knows,
Than my Redeemer's blood.

Faith too, the blood receiving grace,
From the same hand we gain
Else, sweetly as it suits our case,
That gift had been in vain.

Till thou thy teaching pow'r apply,
Our hearts refuse to see;
And weak, as a distempered eye,
Shut out the view of thee.

Blind to the merits of thy Son,
What misery we endure!
Yet fly that hand, from which alone,
We could expect a cure.

We praise thee, and would praise thee more,
To thee our all we owe;
The precious Savior, and the pow'r
That makes him precious too.

Hymn 81
William Cowper
Grace and Providence.

Almighty King! whose wondrous hand,
Supports the weight of sea and land;
Whose grace is such a boundless store,
No heart shall break that sighs for more.

Thy Providence supplies my food,
And 'tis thy blessing makes it good;
My soul is nourished by thy word,
Let soul and body praise the Lord.

My streams of outward comfort came
From him, who built this earthly frame;
Whate'er I want his bounty gives,
By whom my soul for ever lives.

Either his hand preserves from pain,
Or, if I feel it, heals again;
From Satan's malice shields my breast,
Or overrules it for the best.

Forgive the song that falls so low
Beneath the gratitude I owe!
It means thy praise, however poor,
An angel's song can do no more.

Hymn 82
John Newton
Praise for redeeming love.

Let us love, and sing, and wonder,
Let us praise the Savior's name!
He has hushed the Law's loud thunder,
He has quenched mount Sinai's flame:
He has washed us with his blood,
He has brought us nigh to God.

Let us love the Lord who bought us,
Pitied us when enemies;
Called us by his grace, and taught us,
Gave us ears, and gave us eyes:
He has washed us with his blood,
He presents our souls to God.

Let us sing though fierce temptations
Threaten hard to hear us down
For the Lord, our strong salvation,
Rev 2:10
Holds in view the conqu'rors crown:
He who washed us with his blood,
Soon will bring us home to GOD.

Let us wonder, grace and justice,
Join and point to mercy's store;
When through grace in CHRIST our trust is,
Justice smiles; and asks no more:
He who washed us with his blood,
Has secured our way to God.

Let us praise, and join the chorus
Of the saints, enthroned on high;
Here they trusted him before us,
Now their praises fill the sky:
Rev 5:9
"Thou hast washed us with thy blood,
Thou art worthy, Lamb of GOD!"

Olney Hymns

Hark! the name of JESUS, sounded
Loud, from golden harps above!
LORD, we blush, and are confounded,
Faint our praises, cold our love!
Wash our souls and songs with blood,
For by thee we come to GOD.

Hymn 83
William Cowper
I will praise the Lord at all times.

Winter has a joy for me,
While the Savior's charms I read,
Lowly, meek, from blemish free,
In the snow-drop's pensive head.

Spring returns, and brings along
Life-invigorating suns:
Hark! the turtle's plaintive song,
Seems to speak his dying groans!

Summer has a thousand charms,
All expressive of his worth;
'Tis his sun that lights and warms,
His the air that cools the earth.

What, has autumn left to say
Nothing, of a Savior's grace?
Yes, the beams of milder day
Tell me of his smiling face.

Light appears with early dawn
While the sun makes haste to rise,
See his bleeding beauties, drawn
On the blushes of the skies.

Evening, with a silent pace,
Slowly moving in the west,
Shows an emblem of his grace,
Points to an eternal rest.

Hymn 84
John Newton
Perseverance.

Rejoice, believer, in the LORD
Who makes your cause his own;
The hope that's built upon his word,
Can ne'er be overthrown.

Though many foes beset your road,
And feeble is your arm;
Your life is hid with CHRIST in GOD
Col 3:3
Beyond the reach of harm.

Weak as you are, you shall not faint,
Or fainting shall not die;
JESUS, the strength of every saint,
Isa 40:29
Will aid you from on high.

Though sometimes unperceived by sense,
Faith sees him always near;
A Guide, a Glory, a Defence,
Then what have you to fear?

As surely as he overcame,
And triumphed once for you;
So surely you, that love his name,
Shall triumph in him too.

Hymn 85
John Newton
Salvation.

Salvation! what a glorious plan,
How suited to our need!
The grace that raises fallen man,
Is wonderful indeed!

'Twas wisdom formed the vast design,
To ransom us when lost;
And love's unfathomable mine
Provided all the cost.

Strict Justice, with approving look,
The holy cov'nant sealed;
And Truth, and Power, undertook
The whole should be fulfilled.

Truth, Wisdom, Justice, Pow'r and Love,
In all their glory shone;
When JESUS left the courts above,
And died to save his own.

Truth, Wisdom, Justice, Pow'r and Love,
Are equally displayed;
Now JESUS reigns enthroned above,
Our Advocate and Head.

Now sin appears deserving death,
Most hateful and abhorred;
And yet the sinner lives by faith,
And dares approach the LORD.

Hymn 86
John Newton
Reigning grace.

Now may the LORD reveal his face,
And teach our stamm'ring tongues
To make his sovereign, reigning grace,
Rom 5:21
The subject of our songs:
No sweeter subject can invite
A sinner's heart to sing;
Or more display the glorious right
Of our exalted King.

This subject fills the starry plains
With wonder, joy, and love;
And furnishes the noblest strains
For all the harps above:
While the redeemed in praise combine
To grace upon the throne;
Rev 5:9,12
Angels in solemn chorus join,
And make the theme their own.

Grace reigns, to pardon crimson sins,
To melt the hardest hearts;
And from the work it once begins,
Php 1:6
It never more departs.
The world and Satan strive in vain,
Against the chosen few;
Rom 8:35-39
Secured by grace's conqu'ring reign,
They all shall conquer too.

Grace tills the soil, and sows the seeds,
Provides the sun and rain;
Till from the tender blade proceeds
The ripened harvest grain.
'Twas grace that called our souls at first,
By grace thus far we're come,
And grace will help us through the worst,
And lead us safely home.

John Newton

LORD, when this changing life is past
If we may see thy face;
How shall we praise, and love, at last,
And sing the reign of grace!
Ps 115:1
Yet let us aim while here below
Thy mercy to display;
And own at least the debt we owe,
Although we cannot pay.

Hymn 87
John Newton
Praise to the Redeemer.

Prepare a thankful song
To the Redeemer's name
His praises should employ each tongue
And every heart inflame!

He laid his glory by,
And dreadful pains endured;
That rebels, such as you and I,
From wrath might he secured.

Upon the cross he died,
Our debt of sin to pay;
The blood and water from his side
Wash guilt and filth away.

And now he pleading stands
For us, before the throne;
And answers all the Law's demands,
With what himself hath done.

He sees us, willing slaves
To sin, and Satan's pow'r;
But, with an outstretched arm, he saves,
In his appointed hour.

The Holy Ghost he sends.
Our stubborn souls to move;
To make his enemies his friends,
And conquer them by love.

The love of sin departs,
The life of grace takes place,
Soon as his voice invites our hearts
To rise and seek his face.

The world and Satan rage,
But he their pow'r controls;
His wisdom, love, and truth, engage
Protection for our souls.

John Newton

Though pressed, we will not yield,
But shall prevail at length,
For Jesus is our sun and shield,
Our righteousness and strength.
Assured that CHRIST our king,
Will put our foes to flight;
We, on the field of battle, sing
And triumph, while we fight.

Hymn 88
John Newton
Man by nature, grace and glory.

Lord, what is man! extremes how wide,
In this mysterious nature join!
The flesh, to worms and dust allied,
The soul, immortal and divine!

Divine at first, a holy flame
Kindled by the Almighty's breath;
Till, stained by sin, it soon became
The seat of darkness, strife, and death,

But JESUS, O! amazing grace!
Assumed our nature as his own,
Obeyed and suffered in our place,
Then took it with him to his throne.

Now what is man, when grace reveals
The virtue of a Savior's blood?
Again a life divine he feels,
Despises earth, and walks with God.

And what, in yonder realms above,
Is ransomed man ordained to be?
With honor, holiness, and love,
No seraph more adorned than he.

Nearest the throne, and first in song,
Man shall his hallelujahs raise
While wond'ring angels round him throng,
And swell the chorus of his praise.

VIII. SHORT HYMNS: BEFORE SERMON

Hymn 89
John Newton

Confirm the hope thy word allows,
Behold us waiting to be fed;
Bless the provisions of thy house,
And satisfy thy poor with bread:
Drawn by thine invitation, LORD,
Athirst and hungry we are come;
Now from the fullness of thy word,
Feast us, and send us thankful home.

Hymn 90
John Newton

Now, LORD, inspire the preacher's heart,
And teach his tongue to speak;
Food to the hungry soul impart,
And cordials to the weak.

Furnish us all with light and pow'rs
To walk in Wisdom's ways;
So shall the benefit be ours,
And thou shalt have the praise.

Hymn 91
John Newton

Thy promise, LORD, and thy command
Have brought us here today;
And now, we humbly waiting stand
To hear what thou wilt say.
Ps 85:8

Meet us, we pray, with words of peace,
And fill our hearts with love;
That from our follies we may cease,
And henceforth faithful prove.

Hymn 92
John Newton

Hungry, and faint, and poor,
Behold us, LORD, again
Assembled at thy mercies door,
Thy bounty to obtain.

Thy word invites us nigh
Or we must starve indeed;
For we no money have to buy,
No righteousness to plead.

The food our spirits want
Thy hand alone can give;
Oh, hear the prayer of faith, and grant
That we may eat, and live.

Hymn 93
John Newton
Psalm 106:4,5

Remember us, we pray thee, LORD,
With those who love thy gracious name,
And to our souls that good afford,
Thy promise has prepared for them.

To us thy great salvation show,
Give us a taste of love divine;
That we thy people's joy may know;
And in their holy triumph join.

Hymn 94
John Newton

Not to Sinai's dreadful blaze,
Heb 12:18,22
But to Zion's throne of grace,
By a way marked out with blood,
Sinners now approach to God.

Not to hear the fiery Law,
But with humble joy to draw
Water, by that well supplied,
Isa 12:3
JESUS opened when he died.

LORD, there are no streams but thine,
Can assuage a thirst like mine!
'Tis a thirst thyself didst give,
Let me therefore drink and live.

Hymn 95
John Newton

Often thy public means of grace,
Thy thirsty people's wat'ring place,
The archers have beset;
Judg 5:11
Attacked them in thy house of prayer,
To prison dragged, or to the bar,
When thus together met.

But we from such assaults are freed,
Can pray, and sing, and hear, and read,
And meet, and part, in peace:
May we our privileges prize,
In their improvement make us wise,
And bless us with increase.

Unless thy presence thou afford;
Unless thy blessing clothe the word,
In vain our liberty!
What would it profit to maintain
A name for life, should we remain
Formal and dead to thee?

AFTER SERMON

Hymn 96
John Newton
Deut 33:26-29

With Israel's God who can compare?
Or who, like Israel, happy are?
To people saved by the LORD,
He is thy shield and great reward.

Upheld by everlasting arms,
Thou art secured from foes and harms!
In vain their plots, and false their boasts!
Our refuge is the Lord of Hosts.

Hymn 97
John Newton
Hab 3:17,18

JESUS is mine! I'm now prepared
To meet with what I thought most hard;
Yes, let the winds of trouble blow,
And comforts melt away like snow:
No blasted trees, or failing crops,
Can hinder my eternal hopes;
Though creatures change, the LORD'S the same,
Then let me triumph in his name.

Hymn 98
John Newton

We seek a rest beyond the skies,
In everlasting day;
Through floods and flames the passage lies,
But JESUS guards the way:
The swelling flood, and raging flame,
Hear and obey his word;
Then let us triumph in his name,
Our Savior is the Lord.

Hymn 99
John Newton
Deut 32:9,10

The saints EMMANUEL'S portion are,
Redeemed by price, reclaimed by pow'r;
His special choice, and tender care,
Owns them and guards them every hour.

He finds them in a barren land
Beset with sins, and fears, and woes;
He leads and guides them by his hand,
And bears them safe from all their foes.

Hymn 100
John Newton
Heb 13:20,24

Now may He who from the dead
Brought the Shepherd of the sheep,
JESUS CHRIST, our King and Head,
All our souls in safety keep!

May he teach us to fulfill
What is pleasing in his sight;
Perfect us in all his will,
And preserve us day and night!

To that dear Redeemer's praise,
Who the cov'nant sealed with blood,
Let our hearts and voices raise
Loud thanksgivings to our GOD.

Hymn 101
John Newton
2Cor 13:14

May the grace of CHRIST our Savior
And the FATHER's boundless love,
With the holy SPIRIT's favor,
Rest upon us from above!
Thus may we abide in union
With each other, and the LORD;
And possess, in sweet communion,
Joys which earth cannot afford.

Hymn 102
John Newton

The peace which God alone reveals,
And by his word of grace imparts,
Which only the believer feels,
Php 4:7
Direct and keep, and cheer your hearts:
And may the holy Three in One,
The FATHER, WORD, and COMFORTER,
Pour an abundant blessing down
On every soul assembled here!

Hymn 103
John Newton

To thee our wants are known,
From thee are all our pow'rs;
Accept what is thine own,
And pardon what is ours:
Praises, LORD, and prayers receive,
To thy word a blessing give.

Oh, grant that each of us
Now met before thee here,
May meet together thus,
When thou and thine appear
And follow thee to heav'n our home,
Even so, amen, LORD JESUS, come!
Rev 22:20

GLORIA PATRIA

Hymn 104
John Newton

The Father we adore,
And everlasting SON;
The SPIRIT of his love and pow'r,
The glorious Three in One.

At the creation's birth
This song was sung on high,
Shall found, through every age, on earth,
And through eternity.

Hymn 105
John Newton

Father of angels and of men,
SAVIOR, who hast us bought,
SPIRIT by whom we're born again,
And sanctified and taught!

Thy glory, holy Three in One,
Thy people's song shall be,
Long as the wheels of time shall run,
And to eternity.

Hymn 106
John Newton
8,8,8,8

Glory to God, the FATHER'S name,
To Jesus, who for sinners died
The holy SPIRIT claims the same,
By whom our souls are sanctified.

Thy praise was sung when time began
By angels, through the starry spheres;
And shall, as now, be sung by man
Through vast eternity's long years.

Hymn 107
John Newton

Ye saints on earth ascribe with heav'ns high host,
Glory and honor to the One in three;
To God the FATHER, SON, and HOLY GHOST,
As was, and is, and evermore shall be.

www.ingramcontent.com/pod-product-compliance
Lightning Source LLC
Chambersburg PA
CBHW031958220426
43664CB00005B/63